The Absolute Beginner's Cookbook

How to Order:

Quantity discounts are available from Prima Publishing & Communications, Post Office Box 1260, Rocklin, CA 95677; Telephone: (916) 624-5718. On your letterhead, include information concerning the intended use of the books and the number of books you wish to purchase.

U.S. Bookstores and Libraries: Please submit all orders to St. Martin's Press, 175 Fifth Avenue, New York, NY 10010; Telephone: (212) 674-5151.

The ^ABSOLUTE BEGINNER'S Cookbook

OR

How Long Do I Cook a Three-Minute Egg?

Jackie Eddy and Eleanor Clark

Prima Publishing & Communications
Post Office Box 1260
Rocklin, CA 95677
Telephone: (916) 624-5718

To George and Don and our eight children

Illustrations by David Shaw & Associates
Typography by Ad Type Graphics, Sacramento, California

Prima Publishing & Communications
P.O. Box 1260
Rocklin, CA 95677
(916) 624-5718

Library of Congress Cataloging-in-Publication Data

Eddy, Jackie, 1931-
The absolute beginner's cookbook.

Includes index.
1. Cookery.   I. Clark, Eleanor, 1934-
II. Title.

TX652.E346   1987   641.5'12   87-2525

ISBN 0-914629-59-X (pbk.)

90 89 88 87   10 9 8 7 6 5 4 3 2 1

Printed in the United States of America

Contents

Acknowledgments

Having friends who enthusiastically and generously shared their recipes and their ideas made the preparation of this book a very happy experience. A very sincere thank you to:

David Brown
Mary Collister
Janice Eddy
Marilyn Ens
Myrtle French
Marg Getty
Marilyn Gilker
Lynn Hagarty
Peg Holmes
Norm Horne

Joan Jennings
Donna Lumsden
Betty MacFarland
Shirley McMurray
Rosemary Marks
Sharon Marriott
Joan Olson
Gailene Shearer
Margaret Brown Tupper

and a special thanks to Marion Parkins and Sue Strain for their help and support.

We would also like to thank Tom and Alan Sterling, our absolute beginners, who read the first draft of the manuscript and said, "No problem, but how long *do* you cook a 3-minute egg?" The answer is simple: If you live in Boston (sea level) you cook it for 3 minutes, but if you live in Denver, or any high altitude, you cook it for 5 minutes!

Let's Start to Cook, But First . . .

Most cookbooks are designed for people who have time to cook and who know most of the basics. These books are large, extremely detailed, expensive editions which make every dish a major production. They are invariably written by professional cooks, purists who would rather die than use canned soups or "instant" anything.

This cookbook was written, as the title suggests, for the absolute beginner — the person who doesn't know how to cook but who still needs to eat. We have made the recipes *simple.* If you can read and can find the kitchen, the fridge, the stove, and the can opener, you are on your way not only to being a good cook but also to earning a reputation as a host or hostess nonpareil!

We are launching you on your cooking career with the easiest, best-tasting recipes in every category you require — dishes for breakfasts, brunches or light lunches, everyday suppers or fancy dinners, as well as snacks for in-between. We have presented a good selection of many old favorites; but lest the reader become bored, we have included enough innovative recipe ideas to capture the interest of even the experienced, seasoned cook.

A very important "trick" in the preparation of a good meal is having everything come out even — all ready at the same time. The easier the recipe, the easier this is to accomplish. We've done everything possible to simplify the preparation of the dishes in this book. We've taken no cooking skill for granted; we've explained everything step-by-step, and we've reduced the number of steps to the minimum.

We've assumed no familiarity on your part with the names of ingredients or utensils. We've taken care to call ingredients by the names under which you will find them at the supermarket, and in some cases we've even suggested particular brands. With each recipe we've listed the utensils you will need so you can see at a glance whether you're mechanically equipped to handle it. We have described or explained (as necessary) all the utensils in a list at the back of the book. If you are stocking up on kitchen equipment for the first time, you will find this list a handy guide to the essentials.

We have both been cooking for twenty-five years, and during this time we have learned many of the shortcuts, which are a boon for the beginner as well as any busy cook. There is nothing wrong with being a shortcut expert; if it tastes good, do it!

We have a few more general points of advice. The use of salt and pepper varies with individuals. Don't have too heavy a hand when a recipe calls for salt and pepper to taste. Add them carefully, tasting as you go until you are pleased with the end result. You can always add more. The experienced cook can usually rectify over-seasoning, but it is difficult for the beginner.

Have a light touch with spices and herbs as well, until you become more familiar with them, *and don't forget the parsley.* It is very important that a dish have eye appeal as well as taste appeal. Parsley and cherry tomatoes are the best garnishes to begin with. You can get into curls, rosettes, and other exotica when you are more comfortable in the kitchen.

Before you actually start preparing a particular dish, read the whole recipe through first. Then assemble all your ingredients and utensils. Then start cooking. We have tried to present the recipes in a detailed and orderly way, warning you in advance, for example, that you will need to use the juice from a canned vegetable that you were just about to discard; but you will have your best chances of success if you have a clear idea of *exactly* what you will have to do through to the end.

You will see that in all the baking recipes, we have told you to turn the oven on right at the start of your preparations. This is very important. Always give ovens time to heat to the required temperature before you actually place the dish in the oven to bake.

Our last bit of advice — learn to accept graciously these words, "That was the best food I ever tasted!"

This book was a real team effort. With eight children and two children-in-law between us, we had built-in testers. They all highly recommend every recipe found on these pages.

Eggs & Cheese

If you want to see
how to REALLY
flip an omelette
turn to page 16...

Boiled Eggs
Poached Eggs
Fried Eggs
Scrambled Eggs
French Toast
Omelette
Eggs Benedict
Toad in the Hole
Eggs in Toast Cups
Sunday Bacon & Cheese Breakfast
Pancakes
Festive Orange Pancakes
Magic Bacon, Onion, & Cheese Quiche
Macaroni & Cheese
Never-Fail Cheese Soufflé

Helpful Hints

1. Store eggs the same way they are packaged in the store, with the small point down; this keeps the yolks in the middle.

2. A little vinegar added to the water when poaching eggs prevents the egg whites from spreading.

3. One-fourth pound Cheddar cheese yields 1 cup grated cheese.

Boiled Eggs

Every experienced cook has to know how to cook an egg. If you have to cook for yourself it is essential to learn how to deal with eggs. There are countless methods of preparation. We will try to cover the major ones in this section, starting with the most basic, the boiled egg, and gradually moving through to the "gourmet" version, which is Eggs Benedict. All of the eggs used in the following recipes are *large-size eggs.*

1 egg, room temperature   **Utensils needed:**
                                     small saucepan

1. Immerse the egg in a small saucepan of cold water.
2. Bring water to a boil over high heat.
3. As soon as the water bubbles, turn heat down so that water stays simmering, or bubbling gently.
4. *Cover* the saucepan and start timing.
5. For a soft-boiled egg, simmer for 5 minutes. For a hard-boiled egg, simmer for 12 minutes. The timing will depend on how you like your egg. And, believe it or not, the altitude at which you are cooking makes a difference! This timing is for a high altitude. A soft-boiled egg cooked at sea level will take a full 2 minutes less cooking time and a hard-boiled egg will take 3 minutes less.
6. When the egg is cooked, drain off the hot water and immediately rinse with cold water to prevent the egg from cooking further. This also makes the shell easier to peel. (Peel by cracking the shell gently against a hard surface.)

Serves 1.

Note: If you inadvertently overcook your egg, use it to make a delicious Egg Salad Sandwich (see page 57).

Poached Eggs

1 teaspoon white vinegar
1 egg

Utensils needed:
small saucepan
slotted spoon

1. Fill a small saucepan two-thirds full with water. Add vinegar.
2. Bring water to a boil over high heat.
3. When water is boiling, take a spoon and stir so the water moves in a gently circular motion. There will be an indentation in the center of the water — that is where you will drop the egg when you have cracked it open.
4. Crack the egg by hitting it sharply across its widest part on the side of the saucepan. Drop the egg into the swirling water.
5. Turn the heat down to simmer and cook the egg for 2 or 3 minutes, until the white part is solid.
6. Remove the egg with a slotted spoon, holding it above the saucepan for a couple of seconds so the water can drip off.

Serves 1.

Fried Eggs

1 tablespoon butter
1 egg
½ teaspoon water
salt and pepper

Utensils needed:
small fry pan
spatula

1. Place fry pan over low to medium heat and add butter. When it has melted, the butter should cover the bottom of the pan generously. Add more butter if necessary. Heat butter until it starts to foam.

2. Immediately break the egg into the skillet. As soon as the white is set, tilt the skillet a bit and, using a spoon, collect some of the butter and spoon over the egg two or three times so that the top cooks as well.

3 If you like the yolk fairly well cooked, add the 1/2 teaspoon of water and immediately place a lid over the pan. This will reflect the heat onto the top of the egg.
(*Note:* Instead of adding the water, you may turn the egg over gently with a spatula. However, you may find it difficult to do this without breaking the yolk; especially for beginner cooks, this is *not* an easy over!)

4. Remove the egg to a *warm* plate, and sprinkle with salt and pepper just before serving.

Serves 1.

Scrambled Eggs

2 eggs
salt and pepper
1 tablespoon butter

Utensils needed:
small deep bowl
small fry pan
egg beater, whisk, or fork
spatula

1. Break the eggs into a bowl, sprinkle with salt and pepper to taste, and beat with an egg beater, a wire whisk, or a fork until very well mixed.
2. Melt butter over low heat in a small fry pan (no larger than 8 inches).
3. Add the eggs to the fry pan and stir constantly with the spatula as they cook and thicken so the butter and the eggs mix well. The longer you cook them, the drier they become. Most people find them more palatable if they are more on the moist side rather than dry, so remove them when they still are a little shiny on top.
4. Remove to a warm plate.

Serves 1.

Suggested Accompaniments: Midweek — toast and jam. Weekend — bacon and sausage, cherry tomatoes or broiled tomato halves, muffins.

French Toast

1 egg
1 teaspoon milk
1 to 1½ slices white bread
1½ teaspoons butter

Utensils needed:
shallow bowl
small fry pan
egg beater or whisk
spatula

1. Break the egg into a shallow bowl and add milk. Beat well with a whisk or egg beater.
2. Dip bread in egg mixture, making sure both sides get covered with egg. Let moisture soak in a bit, but not enough that the bread starts to fall apart.
3. Melt butter over medium heat in the fry pan.
4. Fry the soaked bread in the fry pan until golden brown on the bottom. Turn with a spatula and cook the other side until golden brown.

Serves 1.

Serving Suggestion: You may sprinkle the French toast with a mixture of equal amounts of sugar and cinnamon, or serve with maple syrup.

Omelette

The secret of a good omelette is speed and constant attention.

2 eggs
2 teaspoons cold water
sprinkle of salt
sprinkle of pepper
1 tablespoon butter

Utensils needed:
small bowl
wire whisk or fork
medium non-stick fry pan or
   omelette pan
spatula

1. Place the fry pan over medium heat.
2. Set your serving plate in the oven to warm.
3. Break the eggs into a bowl and add water, salt, and pepper.
4. Beat the eggs well with the whisk or a fork until there is a high froth on top.
5. Spear the butter with a fork. Touch the hot pan with the butter, which should sizzle on contact. When all the butter is melted, tip and roll the fry pan so that the butter flows over the bottom and part-way up the sides.
6. *Immediately* pour the eggs in all at once; working quickly, shake the pan vigorously back and forth three or four times with your left hand.
7. Prick the middle of the omelette three or four times with a fork held in your right hand, then go all around the edges gently with the fork, tilting the pan with your left hand to allow the uncooked part to flow down underneath (where the heat is). Continue this procedure until there is no more "runny" egg. (If you're left-handed, switch hands!)
8. With a broad spatula, lift one-half of the omelette and flip over onto second half. Now gently nudge or slide the folded omelette onto the warm serving plate.

Serves 1.

Serving Suggestion: You may dress up the omelette any way you like — with chopped ham, cheese, bacon, mushrooms, etc. — by placing the filling (chopped small to heat quickly) down the center of the omelette just before you fold it over.

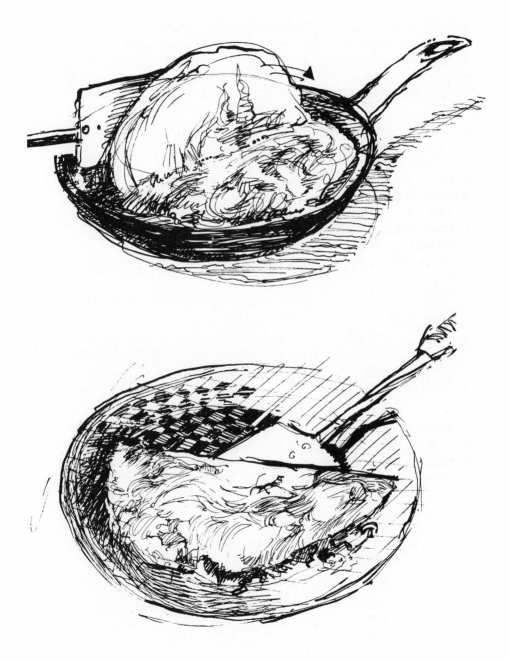

Eggs Benedict

For your first venture into this dish, you should use a Hollandaise sauce mix; most supermarkets carry this, and you simply follow directions on the package. If you want to make your own, however, the (Almost) Hollandaise Sauce that is found on the opposite page is an excellent substitute for the tricky real thing!

2 English muffins, split
1 tablespoon butter
2 teaspoons oil
4 slices Canadian back bacon
4 poached eggs — see
   page 12
Hollandaise sauce —
   packaged mix or
   recipe below

Utensils needed:
medium fry pan
large saucepan
small saucepan
slotted spoon

1. Turn broiler on.
2. Butter muffin halves and broil about 4 to 6 inches from heat until golden brown.
3. Heat the oil in the fry pan and add bacon. Cook over medium heat until the bacon starts to brown, turn, and gently brown the other side.
4. Place bacon on muffin halves and keep warm.
5. Bring water for poached eggs to a boil in a large saucepan.
6. While water is heating, make the Hollandaise sauce.
7. Prepare the poached eggs. (See page 12.)
8. Place drained poached eggs on top of bacon slices and spoon Hollandaise sauce on top.

Serves 2.

Note: For a very attractive garnish, decorate the plate with two or three cherry tomatoes and a sprig of parsley.

(Almost) Hollandaise Sauce

¾ cup mayonnaise
¼ cup sour cream
1 teaspoon lemon juice
½ teaspoon Dijon mustard
sprinkle of salt
sprinkle of pepper

Utensils needed:
small saucepan

1. Combine all the ingredients in a small saucepan.
2. When well mixed, heat gently over very low heat. The mixture does not need to be cooked, just heated.

Toad in the Hole

This makes an excellent supper dish.

1 pound breakfast sausages
¾ cup all-purpose flour
½ teaspoon salt
1 cup milk
2 eggs

Utensils needed:
2 small bowls
8″ square baking dish

1. Place sausages in the baking dish and place in *cold* oven.
2. Turn the oven on to 450 degrees.
3. Combine flour and salt in a bowl.
4. While the oven is heating, beat together the eggs and milk in the second bowl. Add this mixture to the flour and salt, and beat well with a fork.
5. When oven is at the required temperature (usually ranges have a red light that goes off to indicate this), remove the dish from the oven, pour off 1 tablespoon of fat and turn sausages over.
6. Pour the batter over the sausages while sausages and pan are still hot. Return pan to oven.
7. Reduce oven temperature to 425 degrees and bake for 30 to 35 minutes. The batter will puff up, will be brown and crusty, and should be served at once.

Serves 3 to 4.

Suggested Accompaniments: A tossed green salad or corn would complete this meal perfectly.

Eggs in Toast Cups

The cups may be made a few days in advance, making this a very easy dish. When the eggs are cooked, remove them to a warm plate and surround with cooked ham, bacon, or sausages — and don't forget the sprig of parsley!

2 thin slices sandwich bread **Utensils needed:**
melted butter or margarine **muffin tins or custard cups**
2 eggs, room temperature

1. Turn oven on to 325 degrees.
2. Trim crusts from bread, and brush both sides with melted butter.
3. Place bread firmly in muffin cups. Bake at 325 degrees for 15 minutes or until bread cups are golden brown. Remove from oven.
4. Just before you are ready to serve, heat the oven to 350 degrees.
5. Reheat the baskets slightly if you have made them ahead. Break an egg into each warm toast cup.
6. Bake for 15 minutes. (If you have taken the eggs directly from the refrigerator, allow an extra 2 to 3 minutes.)

Serves 2.

Variation

An alternative to the melted butter is a combination of equal portions of soft butter and mayonnaise. Spread mixture on one side of bread only. When you are placing in muffin tins, have the spread side *down*. Bake as above.

Sunday Bacon & Cheese Breakfast

This needn't be specifically for Sundays, nor breakfasts. Add a tossed green salad and it makes an excellent brunch or supper dish.

4 slices bacon
4 slices white bread
butter or margarine
1½ cups grated sharp
   Cheddar cheese
1 cup skim milk
1 beaten egg
½ teaspoon seasoned salt
⅛ teaspoon white pepper
1 tablespoon grated onion
1 teaspoon Worcestershire
   sauce

Utensils needed:
medium fry pan
grater
small bowl
9" x 5" loaf pan

1. Cook the bacon and set aside.
2. Toast the bread, butter it, and cut lengthwise into thirds.
3. Sprinkle one-third of the grated cheese over the bottom of a loaf pan; place 6 fingers of toast on top of the cheese. Sprinkle the second third of the cheese on top of the toast and lay the remaining 6 fingers of toast on top. Sprinkle the rest of the cheese over this.
4. Combine the remaining ingredients, except for bacon, in a small bowl. Pour over the toast and cheese in the pan.
5. Break the cooked bacon into bits, and sprinkle on top.
6. Let stand for 15 to 20 minutes.
7. Turn oven on to 375 degrees and when oven is ready (indicator light will go off) place pan in oven and bake for 25 minutes.

Serves 2 to 3.

Serving Suggestion: If you plan to serve this to guests, the addition of a broiled halved tomato would make a very attractive plate.

Pancakes

Our best advice is to buy a package of pancake mix and follow the directions on the package. However, if you have your mouth set for pancakes and no mix in the house, simply follow this recipe. The thinner the batter, the thinner the pancakes. If you like thick pancakes, cut down on the milk a bit.

1½ cups all-purpose flour
1 tablespoon sugar
1 tablespoon baking powder
½ teaspoon salt
1 egg
1¾ cups milk
2 tablespoons oil

Utensils needed:
2 large bowls
large fry pan or griddle
egg beater or fork
spatula

1. Sift the dry ingredients together in a large bowl.
2. In a separate bowl, beat egg, milk, and oil together with a beater or fork, then stir into dry ingredients until almost smooth.
3. Let the batter sit while you prepare the fry pan or griddle.
4. If your fry pan is electric, set it at 400 degrees. For a stove-top fry pan, turn the element to just above medium. Heat the pan. The best test to see if the pan is ready is to drop a bit of water from your finger — the drop should "bounce."
5. Lightly grease the pan with additional vegetable oil (butter will burn), then pour in some batter — the amount will depend on how large you want your pancakes. One-quarter cup of batter makes a good size.
6. When the tops of the pancakes are covered with bubbles and the edges are beginning to look dry, turn the pancakes over with a spatula. They will take only half the time to cook on the second side.
7. Serve with syrup of your choice.

Serves 4.

Variations

For blueberry pancakes — sprinkle a few fresh *or* frozen blueberries on top of the uncooked side of the pancake before you turn it. Don't add blueberries to the batter when you are mixing it — the batter will turn blue!

Festive Orange Pancakes

1 cup regular pancake mix
1 cup cereal cream
  (half and half)
1 beaten egg
¼ cup frozen orange juice,
  thawed but not diluted

Utensils needed:
medium bowl
large fry pan
small saucepan
spatula

1. Combine pancake mix, cream, egg, and orange juice in the mixing bowl, stirring until smooth.
2. Cook pancakes as described in the preceding recipe (Pancakes).
3. Serve with the following syrup and with crisp bacon or sausages.

Orange Syrup

½ cup frozen orange juice*
1 cup sugar
½ cup butter

1. Combine the orange juice, sugar, and butter in a small saucepan.
2. Bring to a boil and boil for 1 full minute.
3. Pour warm over pancakes.

Serves 3 to 4.

Variation

If you are not watching your calories too closely and are feeling a bit adventurous, spread a bit of sour cream in the center of the pancakes and roll them up, like a crêpe. Should you choose to do this, make the pancakes a little larger, 5 to 6 inches in diameter, and make the batter a little thinner by stirring in an additional tablespoon of cereal cream.

* This is the remainder of a 6-ounce can after you have used 1/4 cup for the pancake batter.

Magic Bacon, Onion, & Cheese Quiche

We've called this magic because you don't have to be bothered rolling out a crust; you simply add the ingredients in the proper order and the crust mysteriously goes to the bottom and the filling rises to the top.

6 strips bacon
1 small bunch green onions
1 cup grated Cheddar cheese
1½ cups milk
¾ cup Bisquick baking mix
3 eggs
1 teaspoon salt
¼ teaspoon pepper

Utensils needed:
grater
10″ pie plate
large fry pan
large bowl
hand mixer or blender

1. Heat oven to 400 degrees.
2. Lightly grease the pie plate.
3. In the fry pan, fry the bacon until crisp. Crumble.
4. Chop the onions, using all the white and a bit of the green.
5. Spread onions, cheese, and bacon in the bottom of the pie plate.
6. Combine the milk, Bisquick, eggs, salt, and pepper in a mixing bowl. Beat for 1 minute with a hand mixer until smooth. (You may pour these ingredients into a blender if you have one and mix at high speed for 15 seconds.)
7. Pour into the pie plate.
8. Bake about 30 to 35 minutes until golden brown and a knife inserted into the center comes out clean.
9. Let stand for 5 minutes before cutting.

Serves 6.

Macaroni & Cheese

This is a dish your mother made you eat when you were a child; but you never really liked it until you grew up, and now you just "have to have some" every once in a while!

2 teaspoons salt
1 teaspoon oil
1 package ready-cut macaroni
  (8 oz.)
1 can Cheddar cheese soup
  (10 oz.)
¾ cup milk
2 cups grated sharp Cheddar
  cheese
½ teaspoon Worcestershire
  sauce
pinch of dry mustard powder
⅓ cup bread crumbs

Utensils needed:
grater
colander
can opener
large saucepan
2-quart casserole
  or 13″ x 9″ x 2″
  baking dish

1. Turn oven on to 400 degrees.
2. In a large saucepan, bring about 2 quarts of water to a rolling boil, then add the salt and oil. (The oil will help prevent the macaroni from boiling over.)
3. Add the macaroni and cook uncovered at a full rolling boil until tender, stirring occasionally (about 7 to 9 minutes).
4. Drain in a colander, rinse with cold water, and drain again.
5. Grease the casserole or baking dish.
6. In a large bowl or the saucepan, blend the undiluted soup, milk, and 1¾ cups of the grated cheese, saving ¼ cup for the top. Add the Worcestershire sauce and mustard and mix well. Stir in the macaroni.
7. Pour into the greased baking dish.
8. Sprinkle bread crumbs and the remaining ¼ cup cheese on top.
9. Bake for 20 to 25 minutes or until sauce is bubbly and crumbs are browned.

Serves 6.

Note: Crushed cracker crumbs may be substituted for bread crumbs.

Never-Fail Cheese Soufflé

Mention *soufflé* to a beginning cook and it conjures up thoughts of the failure factor and what to do with a fallen soufflé! This one really is foolproof and even though it may lose some of its height when removed from the oven, it loses none of its texture because of the tapioca. Don't hesitate to buy minute tapioca; you will use it up quickly (see Beef Stew, page 87), and we guarantee you will want to make this soufflé again and again.

6 ounces Cheddar cheese
1 cup milk
3 tablespoons minute tapioca
1 teaspoon salt
3 eggs

Utensils needed:
grater
small saucepan
spatula
large bowl
small bowl
electric or hand mixer,
　or wire whisk
soufflé dish or 1-quart
　casserole

1. Preheat the oven to 350 degrees.
2. Grate the cheese and set aside.
3. Combine milk and tapioca in the small saucepan.
4. Heat to a full rolling boil (bubbles break the surface), stirring constantly.
5. Remove from heat and add grated cheese and salt, stirring until smooth.
6. Lightly grease the soufflé dish.
7. Separate the eggs, placing yolks in the large bowl and whites in the small bowl. (See note for how to separate an egg.)
8. With a clean whisk or a mixer, beat the egg whites until stiff peaks form.

9. Beat the egg yolks until thick and pale.
10. Gradually add the tapioca and cheese mixture to the egg yolks.
11. With a spatula, gently fold in the stiffly beaten egg whites, then pour into the soufflé dish.
12. Place this dish in a larger dish containing 1 inch of water and bake in a 350-degree oven for 50 to 60 minutes. The top should be golden brown when cooked. (Do *not* open the oven door until soufflé is ready.)
13. Serve immediately if possible, but the soufflé can be held for 10 to 15 minutes by turning off the oven and opening the oven door slightly.

Serves 6.

Note: To separate an egg, hold it over the bowl which will be used to catch the white and crack the shell in the middle (crossways) by tapping it gently on the rim of the bowl. Immediately turn the egg upright, with the largest part of the shell at the bottom. Remove the top shell, allowing one-half of the white to drip into the bowl. The yolk will stay in the bottom because it is heavier. Now pour the yolk carefully into the empty top shell, which will allow more of the white to drip into the bowl. Repeat this transferring of the yolk back and forth until you are left with just the yolk. It doesn't matter if a bit of the white sticks to the yolk but it *does* matter if even a speck of yolk spills into the white, for then the white will not whip. Should this happen, use an empty shell to remove the bit of yolk. (The yolk will adhere better to the inside of the shell than to a spoon.)

Breads & Muffins

Cheesy Garlic Bread
Whole Wheat Baking Powder Biscuits
Easy Cheese Bread
Whole Wheat Coffee-Can Bread
Potato Chip Bread
Big & Beautiful Blueberry Muffins
Banana Bran Muffins
Cinnamon Coffee Cake

Helpful Hints

1. When baking loaf cakes, let the batter sit in the pan for twenty minutes before baking. This will lessen the size of the crack in the top so typical of loaf cakes.

2. Soft bread cuts more easily with a slightly heated bread knife.

Cheesy Garlic Bread

Everyone has his or her own version of this popular favorite, so here's ours. It's a good idea to cut the loaf a few hours or even the day before, wrap it, and freeze it; you will find it easier to spread the butter on the frozen surface. We always keep French bread halves in the freezer for emergencies.

¼ pound butter	Utensils needed:
1 clove garlic	garlic press
1 loaf French bread	small bowl
processed cheese slices	bread knife

1. Several hours or the day before you wish to serve the bread, prepare a garlic butter as follows: Take the butter out of the refrigerator and let it stand at room temperature in a small bowl to soften. Peel the garlic clove and put it through a garlic press. (If you do not have a press, simply chop the clove finely.) Mix garlic into the soft butter.
2. Cover the dish tightly and set it aside, not in the refrigerator (you want to keep the butter spreadable). It will take a few hours for the garlic flavor to penetrate the butter.
3. About 30 minutes before serving, cut the French loaf in half lengthwise; spread each side liberally with garlic butter.
4. Toast the bread halves under the broiler till golden brown. Watch carefully that the toast does not burn.
5. Remove the bread from under the broiler. Lay cheese slices along one half.
6. Put halves together to re-form the loaf. Wrap in tin foil.
7. Turn the oven to 350 degrees — no preheating necessary. Warm the garlic bread in the oven for about 25 minutes.
8. Remove from oven, loosen the tin foil, and cut the bread into 2-inch strips. Serve in the tin foil.

Serves 6 to 8.

Variations

Parmesan cheese may be substituted for the cheese slices. Just sprinkle Parmesan on each half of the bread before placing it under the broiler. If you are rushed, substitute 1/2 teaspoon garlic powder for the clove of garlic, mix it into the butter, and spread immediately.

Whole Wheat Baking Powder Biscuits

Hot biscuits, fresh from the oven — sure to impress (even yourself!).

1½ cups whole wheat flour
½ teaspoon salt
2½ teaspoons baking powder
½ teaspoon baking soda
1 cup sour cream

Utensils needed:
medium bowl
sharp knife
large cookie sheet

1. Heat oven to 450 degrees.
2. Grease a large flat cookie sheet.
3. Combine all the dry ingredients in a mixing bowl.
4. Stir in the sour cream. Blend with a fork or your fingers, only until all the flour mixture is incorporated into a ball of dough.
5. Sprinkle a little extra flour on a clean counter top and transfer the ball of dough to counter top. Using your fingers, press dough to a thickness of 3/4 to 1 inch.
6. Take a sharp knife and cut dough into diagonals about 2 inches in width. Place on the greased cookie sheet.
7. Bake in the oven at 450 degrees for 10 to 12 minutes.

Makes about 10 biscuits.

Note: If you're feeling adventurous, for a change of shape use a medium-size tumbler to cut round biscuits. Scraps may be baked as is; they make great nibblers.

Variation

For traditional baking powder biscuits, substitute all- purpose (white) flour for the whole wheat flour. Or use 3/4 cup whole wheat and 3/4 cup all-purpose flour.

Easy Cheese Bread

Hard to believe something this easy can be so good-tasting. It's a favorite for barbecues. May be made ahead of time: cool, slice, butter, wrap in foil, and freeze until serving time, then thaw and reheat.

1 cup grated Cheddar cheese
3 cups Bisquick baking mix
1 cup milk
1 tablespoon parsley
⅛ teaspoon garlic salt —
    optional

Utensils needed:
grater
mixing bowl
9" x 5" loaf pan

1. Heat the oven to 400 degrees.
2. Grease the loaf pan.
3. Combine cheese with other ingredients in a mixing bowl, stirring only enough to blend.
4. Transfer to the greased loaf pan.
5. Bake at 400 degrees for 40 to 50 minutes.
6. When baked, leave in the pan and cool on a rack for 10 minutes before removing the loaf from the pan.

Serves 6.

Variations

Substitute 1 teaspoon dillweed for the garlic and parsley, if serving with fish.

Also delicious with caraway seeds, poppyseed, or finely chopped sautéed onion, so experiment.

Whole Wheat Coffee-Can Bread

½ cup warm water
3 tablespoons sugar
1 package dry yeast
1 can evaporated milk,
  at room temperature
  (13 oz.)
1 teaspoon salt
2 tablespoons oil
2 cups all-purpose flour
2 cups whole wheat flour

Utensils needed:
2 1-pound coffee cans
large bowl
small bowl
wooden spoon

1. Place warm water in a large mixing bowl and stir in *1 tablespoon* sugar until sugar is dissolved.
2. Sprinkle yeast on top and let sit for 15 minutes.
3. In the small mixing bowl, combine the evaporated milk, salt, the remaining 2 tablespoons of sugar, and oil and stir until sugar is dissolved.
4. When yeast is ready, stir down (it will have risen a bit), then stir in the evaporated milk mixture.
5. Combine the two flours and stir into above mixture. The dough will be a little stiff — you might have to use your "paw" to mix in all the flour, but a wooden spoon should do the job.
6. Grease the coffee cans and lids well. (Instead of greasing, spraying the can with a vegetable cooking spray works really well — the bread never sticks. Be sure to spray the lid as well.)
7. Divide the dough in half and place each half in a well-greased coffee can.
8. Place lids on top of cans and wait until the lid "pops." This usually takes 1½ to 2 hours.
9. About 1¼ hours after you have put the bread to rise, turn the oven on to 350 degrees. You want the oven to be ready, as the bread must go in the oven *as soon as the lids pop.* When this happens, place bread in the oven and bake for 45 minutes.
10. Remove from can and let cool on a cake rack. You may brush some melted butter on the tops of the loaves if you want them to have a shiny appearance, but this is not essential.

Makes 2 loaves.

Potato Chip Bread

People are always looking for something a little "different" and beginning cooks are no exception. This loaf is nutritious and can pinch-hit for a starchy vegetable such as potato or rice.

2 cups all-purpose flour
2½ teaspoons baking powder
½ teaspoon salt
¼ teaspoon garlic powder
¼ cup sugar
1 cup finely crushed potato
   chips
1 beaten egg
1 cup milk
2 tablespoons oil

Utensils needed:
9" x 5" loaf pan
medium bowl
small bowl

1. Turn oven to 350 degrees.
2. Grease the loaf pan (or spray with a vegetable cooking oil).
3. Combine all dry ingredients in a medium-size bowl.
4. Combine liquids in the smaller bowl.
5. Stir liquids into dry ingredients to make a soft dough.
6. Empty the dough into the greased loaf pan and bake for 55 minutes.

Makes 1 loaf.

Note: If you plan on using chips other than plain, do not use the salt-and-vinegar variety. The only other flavor we tried was barbecue and it was great. The recipe does not use a full bag; you may like to sprinkle any leftover crushed chips on top of the loaf before baking.

Serving Suggestion: The last time I made this loaf was to serve with a fish dinner. I saved the leftover crushed potato chips to sprinkle over tomato halves, which I placed under the broiler until heated through — about 5 minutes. Sprinkle the tomato halves with celery salt first; it gives them a particularly nice flavor.

Big & Beautiful Blueberry Muffins

1¾ cups all-purpose flour
¼ cup sugar
1 tablespoon baking powder
1 teaspoon cinnamon
¾ teaspoon salt
1 egg
1 cup milk
¼ cup melted margarine
1 cup blueberries — fresh or
  frozen

Utensils needed:
large muffin tins
large bowl
small bowl
wooden spoon

1. Turn oven to 425 degrees. Grease the muffin tins well, or spray with a vegetable cooking oil.
2. Sift together the flour, sugar, baking powder, cinnamon, and salt into a large bowl.
3. In the smaller bowl, beat the egg, milk, and melted margarine together with a wooden spoon, then stir *lightly* into dry ingredients.
4. Gently fold in the berries. (Never overmix muffins — just enough to absorb the flour.)
5. Fill the well-greased muffin tins three-quarters full.
6. Bake at 425 degrees for 20 minutes.

Makes 8 large muffins.

Variations

Sprinkle muffin tops with a mixture of equal parts of cinnamon and sugar before placing in oven.

If you like the "giant" muffins found in muffin specialty shops, use custard cups to bake the muffins. Be sure to spray or grease them well first.

Banana Bran Muffins

It is fairly common knowledge that buttermilk makes the very best bran muffins. Don't hesitate to buy the dry buttermilk mix because you will use it all; believe us, once you make these muffins, you are hooked. They are the best we've ever eaten and very easy to make.

1 medium banana
3 cups bran — the natural
   bran, not the cereal
6 tablespoons cultured
   buttermilk powder
3 cups cold water
2 slightly beaten eggs
½ cup oil
2½ cups all-purpose flour
1 cup sugar
2½ teaspoons baking soda
¾ teaspoon salt

Utensils needed:
large muffin tins
large bowl
medium bowl

1. Turn oven to 400 degrees. Grease the muffin tins well, or spray with a vegetable cooking oil.
2. Dice the banana finely. You should have 1 cup of chopped banana.
3. In a large bowl mix bran, buttermilk powder, water, eggs, oil, and finely diced banana.
4. In a smaller bowl, combine the flour, sugar, baking soda, and salt. Stir together to mix well.
5. Add the second mixture (dry mixture) to the first mixture in the large bowl, stirring just enough to absorb all the flour. Do not overmix.
6. Fill well-greased muffin tins about two-thirds to three-quarters full. Don't use the paper baking cups; they will stick.
7. Bake for 20 minutes.

Makes 2½ dozen large muffins.

Note: The buttermilk powder plus the three cups water may be replaced by 3 cups fresh buttermilk.

Variations

If you don't like the bran and banana combination, substitute raisins for the chopped banana, or even dates — or a combination of raisins and dates — but don't exceed 1 cup.

Cinnamon Coffee Cake

The marvelous aroma that wafts through your kitchen will have your friends drooling. Serve it piping hot from the oven, and make sure you keep the basic ingredients on hand so you can make it up on the spur of the moment. Great for coffee parties, brunches, and late-night snacks.

1 cup sugar
¼ cup butter
2 eggs
1 teaspoon vanilla
1 teaspoon baking powder
1 teaspoon baking soda
½ teaspoon salt
2 cups all-purpose flour
1 cup sour cream
4 tablespoons brown sugar
1 tablespoon cinnamon

Utensils needed:
large bowl
small bowl
electric or hand mixer
9″ x 5″ loaf pan or 9″ square
   cake pan

1. Heat oven to 375 degrees.
2. Beat butter and sugar in the large mixing bowl until creamy.
3. Mix in eggs and vanilla.
4. Mix dry ingredients together in a small bowl.
5. A little bit at a time, add dry ingredients and sour cream alternately to creamed mixture, beating in between additions. The batter will be thick.
6. Mix brown sugar and cinnamon together in the small bowl, for topping.
7. Grease the pan, or spray with a vegetable cooking oil.
8. Empty half the batter into the pan and smooth it out.
9. Sprinkle half the topping over batter.
10. Add remainder of batter and sprinkle with remaining topping mix.
11. Bake at 375 degrees for 30 minutes if using a cake pan or at the same temperature for 40 minutes if using a loaf pan.

Variation

This batter also makes delicious muffins. Fill greased muffin tins two-thirds full and bake at 375 degrees for 15 to 20 minutes.

Soups & Sandwiches

Soups

Combinations
Minestrone Soup
Instant Borsht with Beef
Chicken Bone Soup
Quick Clam Chowder
Corn Chowder
French Onion Soup
Easy Vichyssoise

Sandwiches

Combinations — Hot & Cold
Broiled Tuna on a Bun
Zesty Wieners
Individual Pizzas
Reuben Sandwiches
Ham & Cheese — Hot or Cold
Easy Egg Salad

Helpful Hint

If too much salt has been added to soups or stews, add a potato.
It will absorb the salt.

Soup Combinations

There are some excellent soup mergers, resulting in flavors unlike the canned soups with which people are familiar, so they taste like homemade. We will list our favorite combinations.

1. Combine 1 can of tomato soup with 1 can of onion soup, 1/4 teaspoon of garlic powder, and 1½ cans of water. Heat. Serve garnished with dabs of sour cream.

2. Combine 1 can of tomato soup, 1 can of pea soup, 1 can of water, 1 cup of milk, and 1/8 teaspoon curry powder. Heat and serve.

3. Combining 1 can of cream of chicken soup and 1 can of potato soup with 1½ cups of milk and 1/2 cup of sour cream in a blender creates a very easy and palatable Vichyssoise. (Vichyssoise is a *cold* potato soup.)

4. One can of consommé and 1 can of tomato soup plus 1 can of water produces a nice tomato bouillon. Heat and serve. Garnish with chopped fresh parsley.

5. Combine 1 can of onion soup with 3/4 cup of whipping cream, sprinkle with Parmesan cheese, and call it "Onion Velvet." Heat and serve.

6. If you want to make French Onion Soup in a hurry, combine 1 can of onion soup with 3/4 cup of water and 1 tablespoon of either red or white wine. Sprinkle with garlic croutons, grated Swiss cheese and Parmesan cheese, in that order, and place under the broiler until cheese is golden and bubbly.

7. Combine 1 can of Cheddar cheese soup, 1/2 can of whipping cream, and 1/4 can of flat beer; heat. Garnish with bacon bits or chopped celery.

8. We even have a suggestion for a soup using vegetable juice! Heat V-8 juice; place 1 tablespoon of cooked and crumbled bacon in the bottom of each dish, then add the hot juice and top with 1 tablespoon of Parmesan cheese. Great!

9. Combine 1 can cream of mushroom soup, 1 can cream of asparagus soup, and 1 can crabmeat, drained, with 2 cups cereal cream (half and half) and 1/4 cup sherry. Heat and serve.

Minestrone Soup

For your first homemade, hearty, stick-to-the-ribs soup, try this
with some crusty French (or Italian) bread. A great treat for lunch
or supper on a cold day. This may be made a day or two ahead
and kept in the refrigerator; it also freezes well.

1½ pounds lean ground beef
1 medium onion
1 rib celery
1 large can tomatoes (28 oz.)
2 cans onion soup
  (10 oz. each)
5 cups water
2 tablespoons chopped fresh
  parsley
½ teaspoon thyme
¼ teaspoon oregano
¼ teaspoon sweet basil
¼ teaspoon black pepper
¾ teaspoon salt
½ teaspoon sugar
1 package frozen mixed
  vegetables (1 lb.)
1 jar of your favorite
  spaghetti sauce (14 oz.)
½ cup broken uncooked
  spaghetti, about 2″ lengths

Utensils needed:
large pot or Dutch oven
can opener

1. Cook ground beef over medium heat in a large stew pot or
   Dutch oven until crumbly, then drain off accumulated fat. (If
   you have a microwave oven, put the raw, crumbled ground
   beef in a plastic colander and place the colander in the
   microwave on a plate. The plate will catch the fat that will
   drain off as the meat cooks. Break the meat up with a fork a bit
   before adding to the soup pot.)
2. Chop the onion and celery. If the canned tomatoes are whole,
   cut them into bite-size pieces. Add to meat together with all
   remaining ingredients except frozen vegetables, spaghetti
   sauce, and spaghetti pieces.
3. Bring to a boil.
4. When mixture has reached a full rolling boil, add frozen
   vegetables. Simmer for 30 minutes, *covered.*

5. Add spaghetti sauce and broken spaghetti pieces and continue to cook, *uncovered* this time, for an additional 30 minutes, stirring occasionally.
6. Serve hot. Pass a side dish of grated Parmesan cheese to sprinkle on top.

Serves 8 to 10.

Instant Borsht with Beef

A hearty one-dish meal, so tasty and easy to prepare it's bound to be a favorite. Great accompanied by Whole Wheat Baking Powder Biscuits (see page 32).

1 can sliced or diced beets
  (19 oz.)
2 cans beef broth
  (10 oz. each)
1 tablespoon lemon juice
1 teaspoon dried dillweed
pinch of garlic powder
½ pound lean ground beef

Utensils needed:
blender
large saucepan
can opener

1. Whirl undrained beets in the blender until fairly smooth. If you don't have a blender dice the beets fairly small.
2. Pour beet mixture into a large saucepan.
3. Add beef broth, lemon juice, dillweed, and garlic powder.
4. Bring to a boil over high heat.
5. While soup is heating, form the ground beef into small meatballs by rolling a teaspoonful at a time between the palms of your hands. (Moistening your hands with a bit of cold water will prevent the meat from sticking.)
6. Add meatballs to boiling soup, cover saucepan, and reduce heat. Simmer slowly until meat is cooked through, about 10 minutes.
7. Serve in individual soup bowls with a dollop of sour cream. Sprinkle the sour cream with a dash of dillweed for flair.

Serves 6.

Chicken Bone Soup

A good cook is also a thrifty one, and no self-respecting budget-wise gourmet cook would be caught throwing away perfectly good chicken or turkey bones.

leftover chicken carcass
1 large onion, cut in chunks
3 stalks celery, cut in chunks
4 sprigs fresh parsley
1 bay leaf
½ teaspoon thyme
4 carrots, diced
3 stalks celery, diced
4 potatoes, diced
any leftover chicken meat
salt and pepper

Utensils needed:
Dutch oven or large saucepan
 (6 quarts)
strainer
large bowl

1. Place chicken bones in the Dutch oven or soup pot and cover with cold water.
2. Add onion and celery chunks, parsley, bay leaf, and thyme.
3. Bring to a boil over high heat, then reduce heat and simmer, partially covered, for 3 to 4 hours.
4. Check continually that vegetables and bones remain covered with water. You may need to add water several times during this cooking period.
5. Following cooking time, strain the soup stock into a large bowl. Discard the vegetables and bones but save any pieces of chicken meat and add to the strained broth.
6. Transfer broth back to the original soup pot. Add diced carrots, celery, and potatoes, and any leftover chicken meat.
7. Season to taste with salt and pepper.
8. Simmer gently until vegetables are tender, about 30 minutes.

Serves 6 to 8.

Variation

You may prefer adding ½ cup uncooked rice or 1 cup uncooked fine noodles instead of potatoes. And if you can't get fresh parsley, use 1 tablespoon dried parsley flakes.

Quick Clam Chowder

This delicious, hearty chowder comes from a friend who would rather be out duck hunting than cooking, so you know it'll be fast to fix as well as satisfying.

4 strips bacon
1 medium onion
1 can baby clams (5 oz.)
1 can Boston clam chowder
  (10 oz.)
1 can cream of potato soup
  (10 oz.)
1 can cream of celery soup
  (10 oz.)
2 soup cans of milk

Utensils needed:
small fry pan
can opener
large saucepan

1. Cut the bacon into ¼-inch strips and fry over medium heat till cooked but not crisp.
2. Dice the onion into small pieces and add to bacon.
3. Fry gently until onion becomes transparent.
4. In a large saucepan combine the remainder of the ingredients. Warm over low heat.
5. Add bacon and onions and, over low temperature, simmer for 10 to 15 minutes.
6. Season with salt and pepper to taste at serving time. Garnish with freshly chopped parsley or oyster crackers (optional).

Serves 6 to 8.

Corn Chowder

3 slices bacon
1 tablespoon butter
¼ cup chopped onion
¼ cup chopped green pepper
1 can cream of potato soup
   (10 oz.)
1 can cream-style corn
   (14 oz.)
1 soup can of milk
2 tablespoons chopped
   pimiento — optional
salt and pepper

Utensils needed:
small fry pan
large saucepan
can opener

1. Cut bacon into 1/2-inch pieces, fry in the skillet until crispy, and drain off fat.
2. Melt the butter in the saucepan and add onion and green pepper. Cook over low heat until vegetables are soft, about 5 minutes.
3. Add the undiluted potato soup, corn, and milk. Stir until well blended and cook over medium heat until soup is well heated through.
4. Stir in bacon and pimiento and season with salt and pepper to taste.

Serves 2 to 3.

Note: To serve more people, simply double the quantities.

French Onion Soup

Restaurateurs tell us this is still their most-requested soup. It is fun and not too difficult to make at home, but you must have the proper bowls.

2 medium onions
2 tablespoons oil
2 tablespoons butter
1 tablespoon flour
2 cans beef bouillon
   (10 oz. each)

Utensils needed:
large saucepan or Dutch oven
can opener
wooden spoon
4 oven-proof soup bowls

2 soup cans of water
2 tablespoons tomato paste*
½ teaspoon paprika
¼ teaspoon salt
4 *thin* rounds French bread*
½ cup grated mozzarella
   cheese*
½ cup grated Swiss Gruyère
   cheese
¼ cup grated Parmesan
   cheese

1. Slice onions into thin rounds.
2. On top of the stove, slowly heat butter and oil in the saucepan or Dutch oven. Add sliced onions.
3. Cover saucepan and cook the onions very slowly until they are a rich brown color. This will take about 15 minutes. Stir only occasionally at first, but once the onions start to brown, watch them carefully and stir frequently so they do not burn.
4. Stir in the flour. When it has been absorbed, slowly add the bouillon, water, tomato paste, paprika, and salt.
5. Cover and simmer *slowly* for 30 minutes.
6. Toast the French bread slices. (They must be thin, or bread will absorb too much of the broth.)
7. Ladle soup into oven-proof bowls. Place a piece of toasted French bread on top of each and cover generously with a mixture of grated mozzarella and Swiss cheese. Sprinkle with the Parmesan cheese and place under the broiler until cheese is brown and bubbly. For easy removal of the bowls from the oven, set them on a baking pan before placing under broiler.
8. Serve immediately.

Serves 4.

* Notes on substitution:

If you have no tomato paste, use 1 tablespoon tomato ketchup. If you open a fresh can of tomato paste and have no immediate use for the remainder, measure the paste into 1-tablespoon lots on plastic wrap and wrap tightly into small individual packets. Freeze until needed. So many recipes call for 1 or 2 tablespoons of tomato paste; these are very useful to have on hand.

Instead of French bread, you may slice French rolls. In a pinch, you may substitute packaged croutons — 1 to 2 tablespoons per bowl.

You may want to use all Swiss cheese instead of part mozzarella. The taste will be good, but we find combining the two cheeses gives the right degree of "stringiness."

Easy Vichyssoise

An elegant cold soup, lovely for entertaining.

2 tablespoons butter
1 cup thinly sliced leeks,
   white part only*
¼ cup water
1 teaspoon instant chicken
   soup mix
1 can potato soup (10 oz.)
1 cup cereal cream
   (half and half)
½ cup milk**

Utensils needed:
medium saucepan
blender or food processor
can opener

1. Melt the butter in the saucepan.
2. Add sliced leeks. Fry over low to medium heat until slightly softened *but not browned.*
3. Add water and instant chicken powder and *cover.* Let cook over very low heat until leeks are very soft — about 8 to 10 minutes.
4. Empty into blender or food processor. Add potato soup, cream, and milk, and blend until well puréed.
5. Pour into a large serving bowl. Place in refrigerator and chill well.
6. Garnish with a few chopped fresh chives (if you can find any).

Serves 4.

 * You'll need 2 or 3 medium leeks.
** The milk is a modest attempt to cut down on calories. You may use all cream if you prefer.

Sandwich Combinations

We will list a few of our favorite sandwich combinations. The fillings may be put between slices of toasted or plain bread.

Cold

1. Sliced avocado, crisp bacon, alfalfa sprouts, and mayonnaise. This is best on whole wheat bread.

2. Ham, Swiss cheese, and sliced pickle.

3. Salami, cheese, and very thinly sliced raw mild onion.

4. Sliced cold chicken, tomato, crumbled blue cheese, and mayonnaise.

5. Peanut butter, crumbled crisp bacon, chopped celery, and raisins, or peanut butter and lettuce. (Yes, really!)

6. Liverwurst, sliced English cucumber, and sliced raw onion. This is excellent on rye bread.

7. Last and easiest we call our BC. L. T. Lettuce, sliced tomato, and mayonnaise with bacon chips sprinkled on top.

Hot

1. Grilled cheese: Butter the *outside* of slices of bread, put sliced cheese between the unbuttered sides, and fry over medium heat in a skillet until golden brown on both sides. Peanut butter sandwiches are nice grilled as well.

2. "Christmas Special": Sliced turkey (or chicken), layer of cold stuffing, topped with cranberry sauce, and grilled as above.

3. Pepperoni, sliced tomato, sliced raw onion, and a slice of cheese on top placed open-face under the broiler until cheese is melted. Rye bread is best for this.

4. Kelly's Special Open-Faced: Spread a piece of toast with mustard, top this with lightly fried shaved ham, fried chopped onion — and then a fried egg. Serve ketchup on the side. This may be put between two pieces of toast; if so, break the yolk of the egg when you are frying it.

Broiled Tuna on a Bun

1 can tuna (6½ oz.)
1½ teaspoons prepared
   mustard
¼ teaspoon Worcestershire
   sauce
¼ cup mayonnaise
1½ teaspoons grated onion
2 tablespoons chopped green
   pepper
3 hamburger buns, split
6 slices tomato
½ cup mayonnaise
¼ cup grated sharp Cheddar
   cheese

Utensils needed:
grater
can opener
small bowl
cookie sheet

1. Combine first six ingredients in a small bowl.
2. Turn broiler on.
3. Divide tuna mixture equally between the 6 hamburger bun halves.
4. Top the tuna mixture with a slice of tomato.
5. Combine mayonnaise and shredded cheese and spread on slices of tomato.
6. Place buns on a cookie sheet and, with oven door open, broil about 4 inches away from heat until top is golden brown; it will puff up slightly.

Serves 6.

Variation

If you want to fuss a bit, combine the first six ingredients and, using a package of refrigerator biscuits, proceed as follows:
1. Turn oven to 375 degrees.
2. Separate the biscuits; there will be 10.

3. Roll biscuits into the shape of flat pancakes, on a lightly floured surface.

4. Spoon tuna mixture equally onto 5 of these pancakes.

5. Top with remaining circles and seal by pressing around the edges with a fork.

6. Place on an ungreased baking sheet and bake in heated oven for 15 minutes, or until browned.

7. Serve warm or cold. These freeze well.

Zesty Wieners

This is perfect TV-watching food. It is easy to make and *so* tasty.

Per person:
1 slice of white bread
2 good-quality wieners, uncooked
1 tablespoon mayonnaise
1 tablespoon ketchup
1 tablespoon mustard

Utensils needed:
cookie sheet
small bowl or cup

1. Grease the cookie sheet. Turn oven to 350 degrees.
2. Lay slices of bread on the greased cookie sheet.
3. Split wieners lengthwise and lay flat on top of bread.
4. Mix remaining ingredients and spread on top of wieners.
5. Bake uncovered for 15 minutes.

Serves 1.

Serving Suggestion: This could be served for supper as well by adding a tossed green salad and a vegetable such as corn or peas to round out the meal.

Individual Pizzas

These are very flexible and a good way to use up bits and pieces in the refrigerator, *i.e.*, mushrooms, cheese, ham, tomatoes, olives, etc. Slice whatever you have on hand and place on top of the pizza spread, then put the mozzarella cheese on last.

1 package English muffins,
  split
1 jar or can of pizza sauce
  or spread (7¾ oz.)
½ cup grated Parmesan
  cheese
oregano
1 package mozzarella cheese
  slices (6 oz.)

Utensils needed:
cookie sheet

1. Turn oven to 450 degrees.
2. Spread sauce on split side of English muffins. The muffins may be toasted or plain, and any unused muffins may be saved in the freezer for an "encore."
3. Sprinkle sauce with Parmesan cheese and a pinch of oregano.
4. Top with a slice of mozzarella cheese — just a bit smaller than the muffin because the cheese will spread a bit when it melts.
5. Bake in a 450-degree oven for 10 to 12 minutes.

Variation

You may make a quantity of these for an hors d'oeuvre by using a loaf of party rye bread and following the above instructions.

Reuben Sandwiches

These tasty sandwiches are great to serve to the gang as a late-night snack. You may make them up ahead of time and pop them into the oven just before serving. Don't forget the dill pickles.

12 slices rye bread
butter
mustard — Dijon or a good
  hot variety
12 thin slices lean corned
  beef
¾ cup sauerkraut
6 slices mozzarella cheese

Utensils needed:
knife
aluminum foil

1. Turn oven to 400 degrees.
2. Butter the bread, and spread mustard sparingly on half the bread slices.
3. Put a slice of corned beef on top of the mustard. (You may prefer to use more corned beef.)
4. Spread about 2 tablespoons of sauerkraut evenly on top of corned beef on each sandwich.
5. Top with a cheese slice, the remaining corned beef slices, and then the other piece of bread.
6. Wrap sandwiches individually in foil.
7. Bake for 20 to 30 minutes at 400 degrees.

Serves 6.

Variation

These are also good done on top of the stove in a fry pan. Instead of wrapping the sandwiches in foil, butter the outsides and heat in the fry pan till outside is toasted and cheese has melted inside.

Ham & Cheese — Hot or Cold

Hot is more popular because just the idea of cheese melting over succulent ham seems to trigger the salivary glands.

Hot

Per Person:	Utensils needed:
1 crusty French roll	bread knife
butter	aluminum foil
1 tablespoon Thousand Island dressing	
1 thin slice of ham	
1 slice of Swiss cheese*	

1. Turn oven to 350 degrees.
2. Slice roll in half.
3. Butter halves lightly with butter, then spread with Thousand Island dressing.
4. Place 1 slice of ham on the bottom half of the roll and cover this with a slice of cheese.
5. Wrap bun in aluminum foil.
6. Place in a 350-degree oven for 10 minutes.

Serves 1.

Cold

Ingredients are the same as above but, since it is not going to be baked, add crisp lettuce. Russian dressing may be substituted for the Thousand Island.

* Dofino Havarti cheese is nice as well.

Easy Egg Salad

Per person:
1 hard-boiled egg
2 teaspoons Miracle Whip
sprinkle of salt
sprinkle of pepper
2 slices bread, buttered

Utensils needed:
small bowl

1. Remove shell from egg. (Grasp the egg in one hand and softly tap it all over with the back of a spoon. Gently strip the shell away from the white of the egg, peeling off the clinging membrane at the same time. You may want to rinse the egg under cold water to make sure there are no remaining shell fragments.)
2. Mash the egg with a fork. When well mashed, stir in the Miracle Whip. (You may want to add more or less than we have recommended, depending on how moist or dry you like your egg salad sandwich.)
3. Sprinkle with salt and pepper and spread between two slices of buttered bread.

Variation

A bit of chopped green onion makes a good addition to this filling.

Note: This filling may not be frozen.

Salads

Olympic Salad Tossing

Tossed Green Salad
Favorite Salad Dressing
Caesar Salad
Marinated Raw Vegetable Salad
Spinach Salad
Avocado Stuffed with Crabmeat
Quick Cole Slaw
California Salad (Cobb Salad)
Ichiban Salad (Chinese Cole Slaw)
Marinated Cucumber Salad
Marinated Onions
Favorite Cucumber Mold
Mandarin Orange Mold
Potato Salad
Romaine Wedge Salad

Helpful Hints

1. Cut out the core of a head of lettuce, wash the head under cold water, drain it, and wrap in paper towels which have been moistened with cold water. It will stay fresh and crisp.

2. It takes four people to make a salad: a spendthrift for the oil, a miser for the vinegar, a counselor for the salt, and a madman to stir them up.

3. Dressing should not be added to salad until the last minute because the oil causes lettuce to wilt.

4. For patio entertaining, serve molds in paper cups.

Tossed Green Salad

The star of this salad is usually the dressing, but it must also feature *fresh*, unblemished lettuce. Choose from the following. (Supermarkets usually have the names, plus the price, above each variety of lettuce so you can identify them.)

Boston (or Bibb)
Romaine
Curly Endive
Iceberg
Leaf (all green or, with red
    around the edges, called
    Red Leaf)

1. Separate leaves. Wash lettuce thoroughly.
2. Dry. (If you have a spinner, so much the better; if not, use paper towels.)
3. Store in plastic bags in the refrigerator until ready to use.
4. At serving time, break lettuce into bite-size pieces into the salad bowl. Add dressing* — the amount will depend on how large a salad you make.

If it is to be for a party, use a combination of different kinds of lettuce, and add one or two (or all) of these suggested additions:

croutons
sliced avocado
sliced raw mushrooms
sliced cucumber
small raw broccoli florets

wedges of tomato
crisp bacon bits
cubed Swiss cheese
radishes
very thin slices of mild
    onion, separated into rings

* See recipe on following page for Favorite Salad Dressing.

Favorite Salad Dressing

½ cup oil
2 tablespoons lemon juice
½ teaspoon salt
¼ teaspoon black pepper
½ teaspoon Worcestershire
  sauce
½ teaspoon prepared
  mustard
⅛ teaspoon garlic powder
1 tablespoon grated
  Parmesan cheese

Utensils needed:
jar with lid

1. Place all ingredients in a jar and shake well.
2. Shake again just before adding to salad.

Note: You may prefer to substitute *wine* vinegar (red or white) for the lemon juice.

Caesar Salad

Beginners should not try to cope with making this at the table, which is traditional. Making the dressing ahead and tossing the salad in the kitchen just before serving will make things less confusing.

1 large head of Romaine
  lettuce
1 cup garlic-flavored
  croutons
2 tablespoons grated
  Parmesan cheese

Utensils needed:
large salad bowl
can opener
medium bowl
garlic press
hand mixer, blender, or food
  processor

1. Early in the day, wash lettuce thoroughly, then dry. (If you have no spinner, paper towels will do — just wrap leaves up and press very gently.) Tear into bite-size pieces and store in a plastic bag in the refrigerator until serving time.

2. When ready to serve, empty lettuce into the salad bowl, shake dressing and pour over lettuce, and toss until lettuce leaves are glossy.
3. Sprinkle Parmesan cheese and croutons on top and toss again, only enough to mix in lightly.

Serves 4 to 6.

Caesar Salad Dressing

½ can anchovies
   (2 oz.-size)
1 small clove garlic
1 egg yolk
½ cup *olive* oil
¼ cup red wine vinegar
1 tablespoon lemon juice
2 tablespoons grated
   Parmesan cheese
¼ teaspoon Worcestershire
   sauce
¼ teaspoon black pepper*

1. Drain the anchovies, and cut in small pieces.
2. Squeeze the garlic through a garlic press into a mixing bowl.
3. Mash garlic and anchovies well together with a fork until a paste is formed.
4. Separate an egg as described on page 27. Discard the white, adding the yolk to the anchovy paste together with remaining ingredients.
5. With the mixer (or a whisk), beat the ingredients together well.
6. Pour into a jar and store in refrigerator until ready to serve.

Note: If you don't want to be left with half a can of anchovies, double the recipe and store remainder of dressing in the refrigerator.

* If you have a pepper grinder, do use it. Using freshly ground black pepper greatly improves this salad dressing.

Marinated Raw Vegetable Salad

Most people know about this salad, but maybe not the beginning cook — and he or she definitely should. It is perfect for a buffet. You may vary the assortment of vegetables to suit your taste. The following are just a guide. (Be sure to wash all the vegetables. There might be little "critters" hiding in the broccoli and cauliflower in particular; soak these two vegetables in cold, salted water for about 10 minutes to get rid of any animal life!)

1 head of cauliflower
2 large stalks of broccoli
2 large carrots
1 medium zucchini
2 stalks of celery
1 green pepper
1 small bunch of radishes
¼ pound of mushroom caps
1 basket of cherry tomatoes
1 bottle of Italian dressing
  (8 oz.)

Utensils needed:
vegetable peeler
large plastic bowl, with lid
large salad bowl and servers

1. Separate cauliflower into florets.
2. Peel the broccoli stalks with a vegetable peeler, and cut into bite-size pieces. Separate florets into bite-size pieces.
3. Peel the carrots; slice carrots, unpeeled zucchini, and celery into finger-size pieces.
4. Cut green pepper into wedges and remove seeds.
5. Trim ends of radishes. Wipe the mushrooms (and trim ends of stalks if there are any). You may substitute 1 can of button mushrooms, drained, if you can't get fresh.
6. Place all the vegetables in a plastic container and pour dressing over. Place a tight-fitting lid on container and store vegetables in refrigerator overnight. Turn container upside-down occasionally during this marinating period to distribute the dressing evenly. If you have no more suitable container, use a double plastic bag.
7. Drain vegetables before placing in a salad bowl to serve.

Serving Suggestion: This may be served as an hors d'oeuvre as well. People are much more aware of "empty calories" than ever before and would prefer to snack on fresh vegetables rather than on something encased in pastry (well, *most* people!).

Spinach Salad

This salad is becoming more and more popular, but make sure the spinach you use is nice and fresh.

½ pound fresh spinach leaves
4 slices well-cooked bacon
  (crisp)
1 hard-cooked egg, chopped
  (optional)
  (see recipe for Boiled Eggs)

Utensils needed:
salad bowl
small jar with lid

1. Make dressing and set aside (see recipe below).
2. Trim off and discard any tough stems or bruised spinach leaves.
3. Wash well in cold water (spinach tends to be a bit sandy).
4. Shake off any excess water or pat-dry with paper towels.
5. Tear the leaves into bite-size pieces into a salad bowl.
6. When ready to serve (not a minute before!) toss the spinach with ¼ cup of the dressing.
7. Sprinkle with the crumbled bacon. (If you are adding the chopped egg, sprinkle it on top with the bacon.)

Serves 4.

Dressing:

⅓ cup *corn oil*
2 tablespoons apple cider
  vinegar
2 tablespoons orange juice
1 tablespoon *light* soy sauce
½ teaspoon dry mustard
1 teaspoon white sugar
¼ teaspoon salt
pinch of black pepper

1. Place all of the ingredients in a jar (with a tight lid) and shake well just before using.

Note: Any unused portion keeps very well in the refrigerator.

Avocado Stuffed with Crabmeat

The avocado is rightly touted as being an almost-perfect food — full of essential vitamins and minerals, and delicious as well. A favorite preparation with many is one-half an avocado filled with a bit of vinaigrette or French dressing. For something a bit more "special" try the following.

1 large avocado
2 teaspoons lemon juice
1 can crabmeat (6 oz.)
¼ cup chopped celery
⅛ teaspoon celery salt
1 cup Thousand Island
   dressing

Utensils needed:
sharp knife
small bowl
can opener

1. Slice the avocado lengthwise all the way around and, twisting gently, separate into two halves. Remove the pit.
2. Sprinkle exposed surface of avocado with the lemon juice. This prevents discoloration.
3. Combine crabmeat, celery, celery salt, and 1/4 cup of Thousand Island dressing. Stuff this into the cavities of the avocado.
4. Place on a lettuce-lined salad plate. Pour the remainder of the Thousand Island dressing over the top. A few cherry tomatoes and sprigs of parsley liven the plate up nicely.

Serves 2.

Variations

You may substitute 3/4 cup mayonnaise mixed with 1/4 cup of chili sauce for the Thousand Island dressing. Also, you may use any kind of seafood — shrimp, lobster, salmon. It must be canned or cooked; use a small can, or 1 cup.

Hint: The avocado will sit better on the plate if you cut a tiny slice from the very bottom to "flatten" it. And should you ever be left with one-half an avocado, save the pit to place in the unused half and it will keep very well in the refrigerator.

Quick Cole Slaw

Using sauerkraut (which is really shredded cabbage) eliminates the most time-consuming task in making cole slaw: shredding the cabbage. However, if you like the taste of sauerkraut you may be disappointed, for there is not a trace in this salad.

1 jar sauerkraut (32 oz.)
1 cup sugar
1 cup diced green pepper
1 cup diced celery
1 cup chopped onion
1 cup grated carrot
⅓ cup oil
⅓ cup vinegar

Utensils needed:
colander
grater
large bowl (not metal)
small saucepan

1. Drain sauerkraut well by pouring it into a colander and pressing all excess moisture out with the back of a spoon. Remove pimiento and discard.
2. Sprinkle sauerkraut with sugar. Stir, and combine with vegetables in a large bowl.
3. Combine oil and vinegar in a small saucepan. Bring to boil over medium heat and boil uncovered for 1 minute. Cool.
4. Pour over salad vegetables in bowl.
5. Refrigerate, covered. This will keep in the refrigerator for up to 3 weeks.

Serves 6 to 8.

Note: If you prefer the creamy-type cole slaw and don't mind shredding the cabbage, simply dilute a cup of your favorite commercial-type mayonnaise with a bit of cereal cream (half and half) or milk (about 4 tablespoons) and add 1 teaspoon sugar. Blend together well with a fork. Pour this over a small head of shredded cabbage and toss. You might want to include 2 or 3 chopped green onions and 1 grated carrot.

California Salad (Cobb Salad)

This is found in the better restaurants all over California, where it originated, and is becoming increasingly popular all over North America. It is attractive, tasty, nourishing, and a great way to use up leftover chicken. Keep all ingredients separate until you assemble them into an attractive pattern in the bowl.

1 cup vinaigrette dressing
1 small head of Iceberg
  lettuce
2 tablespoons chopped
  chives
1 large tomato
1 avocado
2 hard-boiled eggs
8 slices bacon
3 ounces blue cheese
1½ cups diced, cooked
  chicken

Utensils needed:
large, wide salad bowl
jar with lid
large fry pan

1. Make vinaigrette dressing (see opposite) and set aside. The dressing may be made ahead of time and refrigerated.
2. Shred lettuce and place in the bottom of a large, wide salad bowl.
3. Sprinkle lettuce with chives.
4. Cut the tomato in quarters, remove seeds (little finger does it best), then chop the tomato into small pieces. Set aside.
5. Peel and dice the avocado. Sprinkle with a bit of lemon juice to prevent discoloration and set aside.
6. Chop the hard-boiled eggs and set aside.
7. Cook the bacon in the fry pan until crisp. When cool, crumble the bacon with your fingers; set aside.
8. Crumble the cheese and set aside.
9. Now comes the assembly. Shake vinaigrette dressing, pour over lettuce and chives, and *toss*.

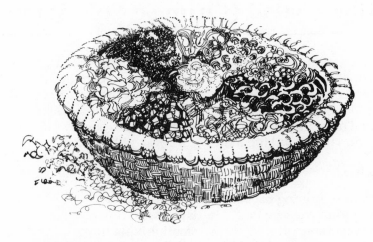

10. On top of lettuce and chives, arrange all the other ingredients (including the diced chicken) in separate wedge-shaped sections — like a pinwheel. The cheese usually sits right in the middle, as the hub, rather than having a wedge of its own.

11. Bring to the table and toss again.

Serves 3 to 4.

Note: You may wish to substitute chopped green onion for the chives and diced Cheddar for the blue cheese.

Vinaigrette Dressing

½ cup oil
2 tablespoons white wine
   vinegar
½ teaspoon salt
¼ teaspoon black pepper
⅛ teaspoon garlic powder
½ teaspoon Worcestershire
   sauce
pinch of dry mustard powder

1. Combine all ingredients in a jar and shake. Shake again just before using.

Note: Use freshly ground black pepper if you can. It has its own special flavor for salad dressings.

Ichiban Salad (Chinese Cole Slaw)

This adaptation of a prize-winning salad recipe in a local newspaper is perfect for entertaining a large group. Even if you don't entertain more than two or three at a time, you are sometimes called upon to bring something to a "Pot Luck" dinner. The next time such an occasion arises, quickly offer to bring the salad. It will be a hit — and you will be a hero!

Dressing:

1 Ichiban seasoning packet
  (from soup package)*
½ cup vegetable oil
½ cup soy sauce
3 tablespoons white vinegar
1 teaspoon sugar
½ teaspoon pepper
  (no salt)

Utensils needed:
large salad bowl
small mixing bowl
medium-size jar with lid

1. Place all of the above ingredients in a jar with a tight lid. Shake well to dissolve the spices. Set aside while you assemble the following:

1 small cabbage, shredded
2 green onions, chopped
½ pound *fresh* bean sprouts
½ pound *fresh* mushrooms,
  sliced
½ cup sesame seeds
½ package chow mein
  noodles (6-oz. size)
1 package Ichiban soup
  noodles (flavor of your
  choice, broken in small
  pieces)*

1. Place the cabbage, onions, bean sprouts, and mushrooms in your largest salad bowl.
2. In a separate smaller bowl, assemble the sesame seeds, chow mein noodles, and Ichiban noodles.

3. *Just before serving*, toss the contents of the smaller bowl into the contents of the salad bowl. When you have tossed these two together, toss with the dressing. (This is a generous amount of dressing. Add two-thirds and then taste. Keep this in mind for any type tossed salad; you can always add more dressing!)

Serves 10 to 12.

Note: One-half cup toasted slivered almonds makes a nice addition to the above salad. The best way to toast them is to place the nuts on a shallow greased baking pan and place in a preheated 300-degree oven until they start to turn a golden brown. Start checking in about 12 minutes. Toss them into the salad with the sesame seeds.

* If Ichiban not available, use comparable brand — usually found in the soup section of the supermarket.

Marinated Cucumber Salad

This just disappears when placed on a buffet table. A good accompaniment to ham or any fish dish.

2 medium cucumbers or 1
   large English cucumber
½ cup vinegar
2 tablespoons water
¼ teaspoon salt
⅛ teaspoon white pepper
3 tablespoons sugar
3 tablespoons finely chopped
   fresh parsley

Utensils needed:
serving bowl, preferably glass

1. Slice unpeeled cucumber as thinly as possible and place in a serving bowl, preferably glass.
2. Combine remaining ingredients and stir until the sugar is dissolved.
3. Pour this dressing over the cucumbers. Refrigerate for 4 hours.
4. Drain slightly just before serving. Don't worry if the cucumbers are wilted; they are supposed to look like that.

Serves 6 to 8.

Marinated Onions

This is as essential to a roast beef buffet as the preceding cucumber salad is to a seafood buffet. Any leftover portion makes great sandwiches when combined with thinly sliced Cheddar cheese.

3 large mild onions
1 cup vinegar
½ cup sugar
1 cup sour cream
1 teaspoon celery seed

Utensils needed:
large bowl

1. Slice the onions into thin rings.
2. Combine vinegar and sugar and stir until sugar is dissolved.
3. Arrange onion rings in a large bowl and pour vinegar-sugar mixture over them. Cover.
4. Let sit overnight or for at least 4 hours.
5. Three hours before serving, *drain well,* discarding marinade. Stir celery seed into sour cream and toss with onions.

Serves 8 to 10.

Variation

One-half cup mayonnaise may be substituted for the 1 cup sour cream. Proceed as above.

Favorite Cucumber Mold

Recipes abound for rich jello molds that are definitely ladies' luncheon fare and seem to be enjoyed mostly by women. So when you are given a recipe by a friend who tells you it is her husband's favorite, don't hesitate to make it for the family or friends. We didn't hesitate and they all loved it. Thank you, Glenn and Sharon!

1 small package lemon jello
½ cup boiling water
2 tablespoons lemon juice
pinch of salt
pinch of white pepper
½ cup shredded cucumber
½ cup minced celery
1 cup sour cream

Utensils needed:
medium bowl
4-cup mold

1. Dissolve jello in boiling water in a mixing bowl, stirring until all the powder is dissolved.
2. Add lemon juice, salt, and pepper.
3. Chill in refrigerator until partially set (*barely* starts to jiggle) — about 30 minutes.
4. Lightly oil the mold.
5. Fold cucumber, celery, and sour cream into the jello and pour into the mold.
6. Return to refrigerator until firmly set — about 4 hours.
7. Unmold onto serving plate. (See next recipe for how to unmold.)

Serves 4 to 6.

Variations

A small can of drained crushed pineapple makes a nice addition. Add this at the same time you are adding the cucumber and celery. Instead of sour cream, you may use yogurt.

Hint: If jello "over-gels" before you add the remaining ingredients, you can always return it to liquid form by placing over hot water.

Mandarin Orange Mold

As a rule, as mentioned earlier, jello salads are enjoyed more by women than by men. However, like the preceding cucumber mold, this is an exception.

1 large package orange jello (6 oz.)
1 cup boiling water
1 small can frozen orange juice (6¼ oz.)
1 cup fruit juice, saved from canned oranges and pineapple
1 can Mandarin oranges (10 oz.) — drain and save juice
1 can crushed pineapple (14 oz.) — drain and save juice
1 cup grated raw carrot

Utensils needed:
medium bowl
can opener
grater
6-cup mold

1. Empty package of jello powder into a bowl and add boiling water. Stir until jello is completely dissolved.
2. Add frozen, undiluted orange juice and stir until melted.
3. Stir in the 1 cup reserved fruit juice.
4. Chill in refrigerator until partially set (*barely* starts to jiggle) — about 30 minutes.
5. Fold in drained Mandarin oranges and pineapple and grated carrot.
6. Lightly oil the mold.
7. Pour jello mixture into mold and chill until firm, a minimum of 6 to 8 hours.
8. *To Unmold:* Run a hot knife around the edge of the mold. Place a chilled serving dish over the top of the mold, then turn upside-down. The molded salad should come out easily, but if it doesn't, dip the bottom of the mold into hot water very briefly, then repeat procedure.

Serves 8.

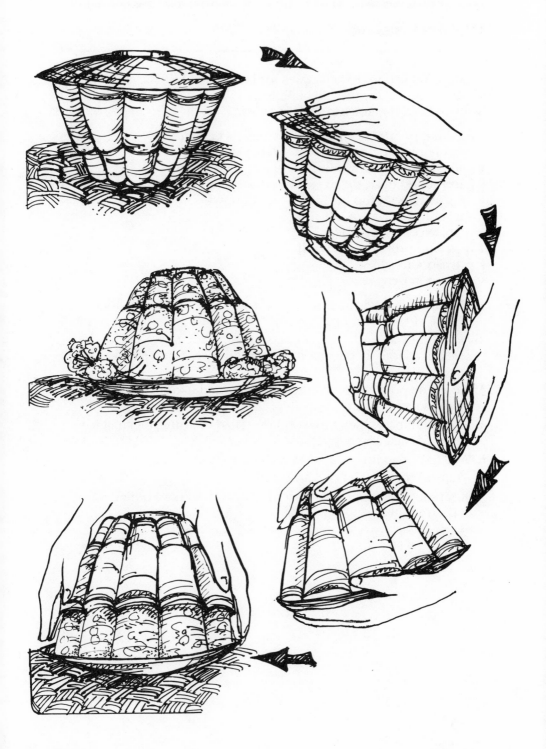

Potato Salad

Potato salad is one of the staples for barbecues, buffets, and hot summer days. Many people believe the best potato salad is made by using cold potatoes, but they're wrong!

5 medium potatoes
1 cup chopped celery
1 cup chopped green onions
4 hard-boiled eggs, diced
½ cup Miracle Whip or
    mayonnaise
¼ cup sweet pickle juice
1 teaspoon prepared mustard
1½ teaspoons salt
½ teaspoon pepper

Utensils needed:
large saucepan
large metal spoon
salad bowl
small bowl

1. Peel the potatoes, then boil in a large saucepan until tender. Drain, but leave in pot.
2. While they are still piping hot, simply hit each potato with the back of a large metal spoon; potato will break into small pieces.
3. Combine potatoes with celery, onions, and hard-cooked eggs in the salad bowl.
4. In a small bowl blend mayonnaise salad dressing, pickle juice, mustard, salt, and pepper.
5. Add to potato mixture and toss lightly.
6. Transfer to serving bowl and chill.
7. Just before serving, garnish with extra sliced hard-boiled eggs if desired.

Serves 4 to 6.

Romaine Wedge Salad

Simple to prepare and refreshingly different from the usual tossed salad. (If you happen to be making this on a weekend, it is a neat trick as you are fixing your morning bacon and eggs to boil a couple of extra eggs and fry some extra bacon.)

1 large head Romaine lettuce
  (or 2 small ones)
6 slices bacon
2 hard-boiled eggs
1 bottle Kraft Creamy Italian
  Dressing*

Utensils needed:
medium fry pan
6 salad plates

1. Several hours or the night before serving, prepare the lettuce: Remove any wilted outer leaves. Cut whole lettuce into wedges; if you managed to find a large one it will cut neatly into 6, otherwise cut small ones into 4 wedges each. Wash lettuce well. Wrap washed lettuce in paper towels, put in a plastic bag, and refrigerate to crisp, until serving time.
2. Fry the bacon until crisp. Cool.
3. At serving time, crumble bacon or cut strips in thin pieces with a sharp knife.
4. Dice the eggs. (If you have an egg slicer, slice the eggs lengthwise first, then turn in the slicer and slice widthwise.)
5. Put a wedge of lettuce on each individual salad plate.
6. Drizzle approximately 2 tablespoons of dressing on top of each.
7. Sprinkle with crumbled bacon, then chopped egg.
8. Serve immediately.

Serves 6.

* Made with sour cream; it is generally found with the produce in the supermarket, and it needs refrigeration.

Main Dishes
Meat

Roast Beef
Roast Beef Gravy
Yorkshire Pudding
Broiled Flank Steak
Easy Shortribs
Oven Pot Roast
Busy Day Stew
Favorite Stir-Fry
Versatile Hamburgers
Meatballs
Make-a-Meal-of-It Meat Loaf
Spaghetti Sauce
One-Step Lasagne
Chili
No-Name Skillet Supper
Pan-Fried Pork Chops
Pork Chop & Rice Bake
Instant Barbecued Spareribs
Pork Tenderloin Casserole
Sausage & Rice Casserole
Sausages Cooked in Beer
"South of the Border" Wieners & Beans
Busy Day Ham Wellington
Broiled Honey'd Ham Steak
Broiled Lamb Chops
Baked Lamb Chops
Liver with Onions & Bacon

Helpful Hints

1. Do not salt meat until ready to cook it. Salt tends to draw out
   the juices.

2. Your roasts, steaks, and chops will be more tender if they are
   at room temperature when you start cooking rather than taken
   right from the refrigerator.

3. When making ground beef patties, add grated zucchini instead
   of bread crumbs. The patties will have a much better texture
   and flavor.

4. If you don't plan to make gravy with the meat drippings from
   a roast, line the roasting pan with foil; this makes cleaning up
   a lot easier.

Roast Beef

You must use a good cut of beef. Standing rib roast is one of the best, and is the cut we suggest. When you are trying to decide how large a roast to buy, allow two servings per rib. The following "cook-ahead" method is the very best method for cooking this roast; it is foolproof. You may cook this in the morning or at noon and forget about it until 30 minutes before you plan to serve it. It would be unthinkable to cook this wonderful cut of meat any way but rare or medium-rare. If you insist on well-done beef, buy a pot roast and follow the recipe on page 86.

3-rib standing rib roast **Utensils needed:**
  (ask for the first 3 ribs) **shallow roasting pan**
dry mustard powder
coarse black pepper

1. Have roast at room temperature. (Four hours out of the refrigerator should do it.)
2. Turn oven to 375 degrees.
3. Rub meat all over with dry mustard and sprinkle fairly heavily with the black pepper. *No salt.*
4. Place the roast fat side up in a shallow roasting pan. Place in oven only when the oven light has gone off to indicate that oven has reached 375 degrees. Cook for 1 hour.
5. Turn oven off but *do not open the oven door for at least 3 hours.* Leave the roast in the oven until 45 minutes before you plan to serve it (time will depend on whether you want it rare or medium-rare).
6. Turn the oven back on to 375 degrees and leave the roast in for 10 minutes *after* the indicator light goes off for rare and 35 minutes for medium-rare. The first cooking (step #4 above) should be at least 3 hours before the second, but the first cooking may be in the morning so there is no rushing home to put the roast on!

Serves 6.

Note: This method may be used on any size standing rib roast. If you like a very lean roast of beef, try an eye of round roast, sometimes called a shell-bone roast. They are usually around the same size, and roasting it in a 400-degree oven for 1 hour produces a medium-rare roast. Season it as above.

Variation — Traditional Method

If you don't want to use the "cook-ahead" method, we strongly suggest buying a meat thermometer and following its guide. You must let the roast sit for 15 minutes when it comes from the oven before carving, to allow the juices to settle. The meat will continue to cook a wee bit from the heat of the roast, so remove it from the oven when the thermometer registers just a little *under* the required temperature.

This is the most accurate method of determining when the roast is cooked. Should you not have a thermometer, use the following timing as a guide.

1. Prepare the roast as for the cook-ahead method.
2. Preheat the oven to 350 degrees — at least 10 minutes of preheating required to reach this temperature.
3. Cook the roast at 18 minutes per pound for rare, 22 minutes per pound for medium, and 30 minutes per pound for well-done meat.

Suggested Accompaniments: Mashed potatoes, Roast Potatoes or "instant" roast potatoes (for "cook-ahead": *just before* turning oven on for the second time, arrange drained canned whole potatoes around the roast, sprinkling potatoes with paprika), Broccoli or Cauliflower and Cheese Sauce, Marinated Onions, Yorkshire Pudding.

Roast Beef Gravy

The easiest way to make gravy is to use a packaged gravy mix or, if you are really nervous, canned gravy — guaranteed not to lump! However, real homemade gravy is very easy to make.

2 tablespoons beef drippings*
2 tablespoons all-purpose
flour
1 cup water
salt and pepper

1. Remove roast from pan and keep warm with foil over top.
2. Pour off all but 2 tablespoons of the drippings and stir the flour into the reserved drippings in the pan until the flour has been absorbed by the fat.

* See step #2 of method.

3. Add water and stir constantly over medium heat on top of the stove until thickened. Add salt and pepper to taste.
4. You may want to add a teaspoon of Kitchen Bouquet for color. This is a browning and seasoning sauce found in the section of the supermarket where you find the ketchup.

Variation

If you have no roast drippings, substitute 2 tablespoons of butter, but then use canned beef bouillon instead of water. You may want to use Worcestershire sauce or ketchup to zip it up, 1 teaspoon of either, or both.

Yorkshire Pudding

You don't have to be from Merrie Olde Englande to love Yorkshire Pudding with your roast beef. It is very simple to make, the only trick being a hot pan containing equally hot drippings. If your Yorkshire Pudding is to accompany Roast Beef but you have only one oven, remove the cooked roast and cover with foil to keep warm while you bake the pudding.

2 or 3 tablespoons fat drippings*
¾ cup plus 2 tablespoons all-purpose flour
½ teaspoon salt
2 large eggs
½ cup milk
½ cup water

Utensils needed:
8″ square baking dish
small bowl
whisk or fork

1. Turn oven to 400 degrees.
2. Put the fat drippings from the roast into the baking pan and place pan in the hot oven.*
3. Combine all remaining ingredients in a bowl and beat with a wire whisk or fork. Don't worry if mixture is a little lumpy.
4. Remove pan from oven and *immediately* pour batter into pan.
5. Bake for 30 to 40 minutes. Do not at any time lower the heat. The pudding must be served as soon as it is ready. Don't worry if it falls a bit — it is supposed to.

Serves 6.

* Instead of drippings, you may use equal portions of oil and butter, enough to cover the bottom of the pan. Heat as above but watch carefully because butter burns easily.

Broiled Flank Steak

This has more flavor and "character" than the more expensive steaks like T-bone and sirloin. It's a lot easier on the pocketbook as well. The flank steak usually weighs around 2 pounds, which is perfect for four people. If there are only two, it makes great sandwiches the next day. This steak, however, must be served rare to medium-rare, as it tends to be a little on the tough side if overdone. If you like well-done steak, you'd better choose a different cut.

1 flank steak (2 lb.)
3 tablespoons oil
4 tablespoons soy sauce
2 teaspoons brown sugar
¼ teaspoon pepper
¼ teaspoon garlic powder
⅛ teaspoon ginger
(no salt)

Utensils needed:
small bowl or measuring cup
9" x 13" baking pan

1. Try to remove as much of the membrane from the steak as you can do easily.
2. Score the meat on both sides — this means take a sharp knife and make slashes on the diagonal about quarter-way into the flesh, then do the same in the opposite direction so you have created "diamonds" about 1 inch wide. Turn the steak over and do the same on the opposite side.

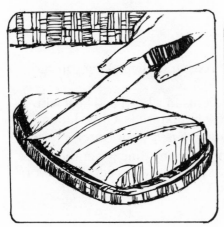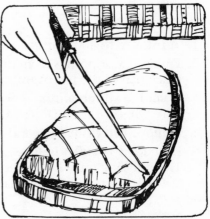

3. Combine the remaining ingredients — *no salt* — and pour over meat in the baking pan.
4. Let meat marinate in this for about 3 hours. (It is not necessary to refrigerate during this time.) Remove meat from marinade before broiling, but save marinade to pour over steak when cooked.
5. Turn broiler on for 10 minutes — you want it well preheated. When broiling the steak, leave the oven door open.
6. Broil 3 to 4 inches from heat for 5 minutes on one side and 3 to 4 minutes on the other; it will be medium-rare. Flank steak should not be too rare or too well-done.

Serves 4.

Suggested Accompaniments: Baked Potatoes, Stir-Fried Broccoli, wedges of lettuce with dressing of your choice.

Easy Shortribs

From a busy bachelor!

3 carrots
3 onions
4 shortribs (lean and
  bone in)*
1 package dehydrated onion
  soup mix (1.5 oz.)

Utensils needed:
vegetable peeler
aluminum foil
  (heavy duty)

1. Turn oven to 250 degrees.
2. Peel carrots and cut in half, lengthwise.
3. Peel onions and cut in thick slices.
4. On about three thicknesses of heavy-duty foil, layer shortribs between vegetables and sprinkle onion soup mix over all. *No salt.*
5. Seal tightly. Place on a cookie sheet and bake for 3 to 4 hours. Turn oven off until you are ready to eat; this waits well in the oven. All the goodness is sealed in the foil packet.

Serves 4.

Suggested Accompaniment: Mashed Potatoes.

* Don't use the boneless shortribs; they tend to dry out a bit. Ribs are much better cooked on the bone.

Oven Pot Roast

An easy main dish, no browning necessary and no gravy to make; it makes its own great gravy.

4- to 5-pound chuck roast*
1 package dehydrated onion
  soup mix (1.5 oz.)
1 can cream of mushroom
  soup (10 oz.)

Utensils needed:
Dutch oven or small roasting
  pan
small bowl
can opener

1. Heat oven to 350 degrees.
2. Place meat in a Dutch oven or roasting pan. (Meat need not have extra space around it.)
3. Mix dry soup mix and undiluted mushroom soup together and pour over and around the meat. Mixture will be thick.
4. Cover tightly with foil or a lid that fits the pan.
5. Bake for 2½ to 3 hours at 350 degrees.

Serves 6 to 8.

Serving Suggestion: This may be made into a complete one-dish meal by adding potatoes, carrots, onions, turnips, or parsnips for the last hour of cooking. (You may have to use a larger roasting pan for this.)

* Other suitable cuts of meat include rolled brisket or blade roast. If the meat weighs less than 4 pounds, use only part of the onion soup mix but all of the mushroom soup.

Busy Day Stew

So easy and tasty. Make it in the morning and be greeted by the pleasant aroma of home cooking when you return later in the day.

1 medium onion
6 stalks celery — optional
3 medium potatoes
6 carrots
2 pounds lean stewing beef
2 teaspoons salt
1 tablespoon sugar
3 tablespoons minute tapioca
1½ cups tomato juice

Utensils needed:
large, shallow, oven-proof
   casserole or crock pot

1. Heat oven to 250 degrees.
2. Chop the vegetables. Cut the onion into small chunks, the celery into 1-inch pieces, the potatoes into quarters, and the carrots into long strips.
3. Combine all ingredients in a shallow casserole.
4. Cover tightly with lid or foil.
5. Bake for at least 4 hours.
6. Once the stew has been cooked, it can stay in the oven for up to 3 to 4 hours; if you will need to hold it longer, add an extra ½ cup tomato juice.

Serves 4 to 6.

Note: Parsnips and turnips are also good additions to a stew.

Favorite Stir-Fry

This is best made just prior to serving, so it is a perfect candidate for a showy "making it at the table" dish, but you must have an electric fry pan or an electric wok. (If you plan to cook it in the kitchen, any large fry pan will do.) Have the meat and vegetables sliced ahead, then it is just a matter of adding them to the pan in the right order. Have the oil and garlic in the pan before bringing it to the table, and have the soy sauce and cornstarch mixed in a little custard cup or other small dish, ready for use. Have the rice cooked and keep it warm in the kitchen until needed.

1 pound sirloin steak
4 teaspoons dry mustard
  powder
2 tablespoons soy sauce
2 teaspoons cornstarch
6 green onions
¼ pound fresh mushrooms
¼ pound pea pods
¼ cup oil
1 clove garlic
salt and pepper

Utensils needed:
electric fry pan or electric
  wok
small bowl or cup
wooden spoon

1. Four hours before you plan to cook the stir-fry, trim the steak of all fat and rub meat on both sides with dry mustard, about 2 teaspoons for each side. This helps tenderize the meat. If you are going to be gone all day, you may do this in the morning, then place meat in the refrigerator.
2. Just prior to cooking, slice steak into very thin slices, cutting across the grain. If you place it in the freezer for about 30 minutes, until partially frozen, the steak slices very easily.
3. Stir cornstarch into the soy sauce in a little bowl and set aside.
4. Trim onions and slice into 1-inch pieces, including some of the green part.
5. Wipe the mushrooms. Cut large mushrooms in half, but leave small ones whole.

6. Cut tips and tails off pea pods and remove any stringy spine — it pulls off like a thread. If you use frozen pea pods, you need not do this, but rinse in cold water just to thaw, then pat dry with paper towels. (The fresh ones are better, naturally.)

7. Place oil and the whole clove of garlic in the fry pan or wok, and turn heat as high as it will go. Stir garlic around for 1 or 2 minutes to flavor the oil, being careful not to burn it.

8. Remove garlic and add beef. Stir beef around over high heat, using a wooden spoon. The slices might stick together a wee bit from the mustard but will separate easily when you push them around with the spoon. Cook the meat, stirring most of the time, until all trace of pink disappears from the surface. This will take about 3 minutes.

9. Sprinkle meat lightly with salt and pepper, then add all of the vegetables and stir with the beef, still over very high heat. Cook for 3 to 4 minutes, stirring most of the time. None of these vegetables needs too much cooking. You want the vegetables to retain a lot of their texture, so don't overcook.

10. Remix cornstarch and soy sauce until well blended and add to fry pan. Cook for 1 minute, stirring constantly until cornstarch thickens and is well distributed among the meat and vegetables.

11. Serve immediately over hot rice.

Serves 2 to 3.

Versatile Hamburgers

So named because you can make either hamburgers or meatballs with the same recipe.

½ pound lean ground beef
1 egg
2 tablespoons oatmeal
2 tablespoons wheat germ
¼ teaspoon salt
⅛ teaspoon black pepper
⅛ teaspoon garlic powder
2 hamburger buns

Utensils needed:
small bowl
medium fry pan
spatula

1. Place all ingredients (except buns) in a small bowl and mix well — get right in and squish well with your clean hands.
2. Form into 2 patties.
3. Place in fry pan over medium heat and cook the patties for 4 to 5 minutes on each side.
4. Remove from the pan and place on toasted or plain, buttered hamburger buns. Add your favorite topping and eat.

Serves 2.

Suggested Toppings: Sliced raw onion, sliced raw tomatoes and lettuce, cheese slices, crisply cooked bacon slices, sliced pickles, mustard, and ketchup are all great accompaniments.

Note: One-fourth cup of bread crumbs may be substituted for the combination of wheat germ and oatmeal.

Meatballs

Use the preceding basic recipe but, instead of forming patties, shape into 1¼-inch balls and place in a baking pan. Turn oven to 450 degrees and when oven has reached this temperature (indicator light goes out), place meatballs in oven for 15 minutes. When done, they should be slightly pink in the center. (To test: Remove one meatball and cut in half.)

1/2 pound ground beef — this is about 1 cup — makes roughly 12 to 14 meatballs. These freeze well and are useful to have on hand. For example:

Quick Spaghetti and Meatball Dinner

Thaw meatballs (take them out of the freezer in the morning to cook them that evening); simmer for about 20 minutes in canned spaghetti sauce. Pour over cooked spaghetti.

Make-a-Meal-of-It Meat Loaf

1¼ pounds lean ground beef
⅔ cup evaporated milk
½ cup bread crumbs or
   cracker crumbs
¼ cup ketchup
2 teaspoons salt
½ teaspoon pepper
2 teaspoons Worcestershire
   sauce
3 medium potatoes
3 medium carrots
2 teaspoons parsley flakes or
   freshly chopped parsley

Utensils needed:
medium bowl
small roasting pan
   or 2-quart casserole

1. Heat oven to 375 degrees.
2. Combine the meat, milk, crumbs, ketchup, *1 teaspoon* salt, *1/4 teaspoon* pepper, and Worcestershire sauce in a bowl; blend really well (hands work best).
3. Shape the mixture into a loaf and place in the center of the baking dish.
4. Peel the potatoes and carrots and cut into 1/4-inch slices.
5. Arrange the vegetables in layers around the meat. Sprinkle each layer with the remaining 1 teaspoon salt and 1/4 teaspoon pepper. Sprinkle top layer with chopped parsley.
6. Cover pan tightly with foil or lid.
7. Bake at 375 degrees for 1 hour or until vegetables are fork-tender.
8. Uncover and bake 10 additional minutes to brown the meat.

Serves 4.

Variation

You might want to try laying 2 strips of uncooked bacon across the top of the meat loaf; it's attractive and flavorful.

Suggested Accompaniments: Tossed Green Salad or Cole Slaw.

Spaghetti Sauce

1 medium onion
1 small green pepper
2 tablespoons olive oil
1½ pounds ground beef
¼ pound fresh mushrooms
1 teaspoon oregano
¼ teaspoon garlic powder
2 cans spaghetti sauce, any
   variety (14 oz. each)

Utensils needed:
Dutch oven or large pot
can opener

1. Chop onion and green pepper.
2. Pour olive oil into the bottom of the Dutch oven (or large pot) and set over medium heat.
3. Add onion and green pepper and fry gently until soft.
4. Add ground beef. Cook until all trace of pink disappears, stirring occasionally.
5. Add mushrooms and sprinkle with oregano and garlic powder.
6. Turn heat to low before adding the canned spaghetti sauce.
7. Simmer, *covered*, for 30 minutes, stirring occasionally.
8. Serve over hot cooked spaghetti. (Follow directions for cooking on the spaghetti package.)

Serves 4 to 6.

Suggested Accompaniments: Caesar Salad, Cheesy Garlic Bread.

One-Step Lasagne

Actually, it's three steps.

Don't be afraid to tackle lasagne just because you are a beginner. This recipe was designed for you and eliminates cooking the noodles beforehand, which most people find the most tedious job of all. (The noodles have a tendency to tear unless you cook them perfectly; they also love to slip into the sink when you are trying to drain them.)

2½ cups grated
   mozzarella cheese
2 cups dry-curd cottage
   cheese
1 egg
1 teaspoon salt
1 jar spaghetti sauce
   (28 oz.)
½ teaspoon oregano
½ package uncooked lasagne
   noodles (1 lb.)
⅔ cup water

Utensils needed:
grater
medium bowl
9″ x 13″ baking dish

1. Set aside ½ cup of the mozzarella cheese for the top of the casserole.
2. Combine the cottage cheese, remaining 2 cups mozzarella cheese, egg, and salt in a bowl.
3. Add oregano to spaghetti sauce. Spread ⅔ cup of this sauce over the bottom of the baking dish. It won't cover every inch, but don't worry and don't be tempted to add more.
4. Place 5 of the dry noodles (this is half the required quantity) over this in a single layer — 4 lengthways and 1 crossways. (The crossways one will be a little too long so cut a bit off the end with sharp scissors.) The noodles won't cover every inch of the pan, but they do swell a bit, and you want a little space around the edges of the pan because this is where you are going to pour the water just before the dish goes into the oven.

5. Place half of the cheese mixture on top of the noodles.
6. Pour another ⅔ cup of sauce over the cheese mixture.
7. Lay remaining noodles on top of spaghetti sauce and top with remaining cheese mixture.
8. Pour remaining sauce over all. Last, top with the ½ cup of saved grated cheese.
9. The uncooked dish can sit all day in the refrigerator, or overnight if you wish.
10. Just before baking, heat the oven to 350 degrees.
11. Pour the water around the edge of the casserole, *cover,* and bake for 1 hour.
12. After removing the lasagne from the oven, *let it sit for 20 minutes before cutting it into serving pieces. This is important!*

Serves 6.

Note: This recipe doubles very well and freezes well after cooking.

Variations

Add 1 pound ground beef to the spaghetti sauce. Cook the ground beef first by gently frying until the red has disappeared. Drain off fat.

Combine 1 package frozen spinach with the cheese mixture.

Suggested Accompaniments: Tossed Green Salad and Cheesy Garlic Bread.

Chili

Our friend Sheilah is gorgeous and has the tidiest kitchen you'll ever see — and why not? — she *never* cooks. Although she has been married for twenty-five years, our Sheilah can still be classified as an "absolute beginner." She does, however, make *one* thing — the best chili — and if she can, we know you can! It makes a large amount, but it's great party fare. You can freeze any unused portions in small containers.

2 pounds lean ground beef
4 medium-size onions
2 medium-size green peppers
3 cans kidney beans, drained
   (14 oz. each)
2 packages (envelopes) chili
   mix
3 cans button mushrooms,
   drained (10 oz. each)
2 cans tomato soup
   (10 oz. each)
2 cans tomatoes
   (14 oz. each)
¼ cup white vinegar
1 teaspoon chili powder
3 dried red chili peppers
1 teaspoon salt
½ teaspoon pepper

Utensils needed:
Dutch oven
can opener

1. Sauté ground beef in Dutch oven or large pot until meat loses its pink color. Drain off any fat that accumulates in the bottom of the pan.
2. Cut onions into large chunks — about 8 per onion. Add to ground beef and sauté until onions turn transparent in color.
3. Cut green peppers in half, remove seeds and discard. Cut each half into large chunks and add to pot. Continue sautéing for 2 to 3 minutes.
4. Add drained kidney beans, chili mix, and drained mushrooms.

5. Stir in tomato soup, canned tomatoes, vinegar, and chili powder.
6. Crush dried chili peppers between your fingers and add. (Do *not* touch your eyes until you have washed your fingers!)
7. Stir in salt and pepper and continue to simmer for about 30 minutes, stirring occasionally.

Serves 12.

Note: We like the "chunky" vegetables, but they are not really typical of chili. If you think you would like a finer texture, by all means chop the vegetables into smaller pieces.

No-Name Skillet Supper

Every busy "old hand" at cooking knows about the following recipe, but it's probably not written down anywhere — it is something children have seen their mothers make, and they just leave home knowing about it.

½ pound lean ground beef
¼ cup chopped onion
1 can of spaghetti
  (any size)

Utensils needed:
medium to large fry pan
can opener

1. In a skillet over medium heat, fry onion and ground beef together, stirring occasionally, until no trace of pink remains in the ground beef. (If the beef was not lean, drain off most of the fat that will accumulate as it cooks.)
2. Add canned spaghetti to fry pan, and stir with the beef and onion until well mixed.
3. Simmer all together for 5 to 10 minutes, stirring occasionally.

Serves 2.

Serving Suggestion: A tossed green salad and hot rolls make this a very simple but filling supper.

Pan-Fried Pork Chops

Chops from the loin are the choicest.

2 pork chops, 1″ thick
2 tablespoons water

Utensils needed:
small fry pan with lid (most
  fry pans do not come with
  a lid, so find one from a
  saucepan that will fit)

1. Trim excess fat from chops.
2. Heat a small fry pan over medium heat and rub the inside with a piece of the fat you have trimmed from the chops, until the pan looks well greased.
3. Brown chops fairly slowly on both sides, roughly 3 minutes each side.
4. Add water to fry pan and *cover* tightly.
5. Turn heat to low and continue cooking for 30 minutes.

Serves 1 or 2.

Note: Thin chops require no water; cover tightly and reduce cooking time to 20 minutes if your chops are thinner than 1 inch.

Suggested Accompaniments: Baked Potato, Carrots and Brussels Sprouts, applesauce.

Pork Chop & Rice Bake

4 to 6 pork chops
1 can cream of chicken soup
  (10 oz.)
½ soup can of milk
1 cup instant rice, uncooked

Utensils needed:
large fry pan
9″ square baking dish
can opener

1. Turn oven to 350 degrees.
2. Brown chops in the fry pan over medium heat.
3. Remove chops from fry pan and arrange in a baking dish.
4. Combine soup, milk, and rice, and pour over chops.
5. Cover with a lid, if your baking dish has one, or aluminum foil folded tightly over the edges to fit snugly.
6. Place in oven and bake, covered, for 1 hour.

Serves 4.

Suggested Accompaniments: Carrots and canned peas (petit pois — the very best canned peas available; some people prefer them to fresh or fresh frozen; just heat and serve).

Instant Barbecued Spareribs

Simply prepared, simply scrumptious. This is one of those good news, bad news stories. The good news is that when we tried these, our families raved, "Gee, Mom, these are the best barbecued spareribs you've ever made!" The bad news was that we had spent fifty years, collectively, laboring over complicated ten- or twelve-ingredient recipes for them before we found this incredibly easy one.

2 to 3 pounds lean back
  spareribs
1 onion
1 cup bottled barbecue sauce
  (your favorite brand)

Utensils needed:
broiler pan or baking pan
  and rack

1. Cut ribs into sections of 1 or 2 ribs each.
2. Heat oven to 400 degrees.
3. Place ribs on top rack of broiler pan. (Most ovens come with one.)
4. Cook ribs for 30 minutes, then turn ribs over and bake for another 30 minutes.
5. Reduce oven heat to 300 degrees.
6. Remove broiler or baking pan from oven, and set the rack with ribs on it on paper towels. Pour out the accumulated grease from the broiler pan.
7. Cut the onion into large slices (if you like onions) or, if you don't want them to be so evident, dice onion small.
8. Add onions and barbecue sauce to broiler pan, then add ribs. Turn ribs over a couple of times to coat with sauce.
9. Bake for 1½ hours.

Serves 4 to 6.

Suggested Accompaniments: Hot Fluffy Rice, Glazed Carrots, green peas.

Pork Tenderloin Casserole

Very good and with very little effort.

2 pork tenderloins, about
   1½ pounds altogether
2 tablespoons all-purpose
   flour
salt and pepper
2 tablespoons cooking oil
1 small onion
1 can cream of mushroom
   soup (10 oz.)
1 can whole button
   mushrooms (10 oz.) —
   drain and save juice
¼ cup juice from canned
   mushrooms
4 tablespoons Burgess
   Mushroom Au Jus*

Utensils needed:
small paper or plastic bag
medium fry pan
8″ square casserole
small bowl
can opener

1. Turn oven to 325 degrees.
2. Cut pork diagonally into 1½- to 2-inch pieces.
3. Place flour in a small bag, paper or plastic, and sprinkle with salt and pepper. Shake pieces of pork in the bag a few at a time to coat with flour.
4. Place fry pan over medium heat, add oil and meat, and fry meat until browned on both sides.
5. Transfer meat to the casserole dish.
6. Chop the onion finely.
7. In the small bowl, combine onion, undiluted soup, drained mushrooms and reserved mushroom juice, and the Mushroom Au Jus. Pour over meat.
8. Cover and bake at 325 degrees for 1½ hours.

Serves 4.

Suggested Accompaniments: Rice, Green Beans, cherry tomatoes.

* Comes in a bottle with an orange label and is available at most supermarkets.

Sausage & Rice Casserole

A favorite because of its versatility. May be cooked on the stove top or in the oven. An excellent dish to accompany barbecued beef. The best feature, though: It doubles, triples, and quadruples for a crowd.

1 pound sausage meat
1 large onion
1½ cups long-grain rice, uncooked
2 cans button mushrooms (10 oz. each)
2 cans consommé (10 oz. each)

Utensils needed:
large saucepan
can opener
large casserole

1. Thaw the sausage meat, if frozen. Chop the onion.
2. Cook sausage over medium heat in a saucepan until well browned. Lower heat, add onion, and continue cooking until onion becomes transparent.
3. Add rice and cook until rice becomes golden-colored, stirring continuously.
4. Add undrained mushrooms and consommé.
5. Continue cooking at a low heat, stirring occasionally, until liquid has been absorbed — about 30 minutes, until rice is cooked.
6. Transfer to a casserole to serve. Decorate with fresh parsley.

Serves 6 to 8 as a main dish, 10 to 12 as a buffet accompaniment. Any leftover portion freezes well.

Variation

If you prefer, after you have added the soup and mushrooms, transfer to a casserole, cover, and finish cooking in the oven, about 35 to 40 minutes at 350 degrees.

Sausages Cooked in Beer

This recipe does not use the entire bottle of beer; drink the rest or pour it over your hair as a rinse!

1 tablespoon oil
1 pound sausages, preferably
  pork
1 cup beer

Utensils needed:
medium fry pan with lid

1. Heat oil in fry pan over medium heat. Add sausages and brown on both sides.
2. Remove sausages to paper towels to drain, and discard fat that has accumulated in the bottom of the fry pan.
3. Return sausages to fry pan and add beer. Bring to a boil, cover with lid, then turn heat to low and simmer the sausages for 15 minutes.

Serves 3.

Suggested Accompaniments: Mashed Potatoes, Brussels Sprouts, Broiled or Baked Tomato Halves.

"South of the Border" Wieners & Beans

This will definitely be a hit if you love Mexican food. If you like it "hot," follow the recipe exactly. If you prefer it on the mild side, try the variation below. This is also a dazzling disguise for wieners!

1 pound wieners
1 medium onion
1 can pork and beans in
  tomato sauce (14 oz.)
2 cups grated Cheddar
  cheese or Monterey Jack
  cheese
1 package taco-flavored
  tortilla chips (5 oz.)
1 jar taco sauce (9 oz.)

Utensils needed:
9″ x 13″ baking dish
can opener
grater

1. Turn oven to 300 degrees.
2. Slice wieners crosswise into 1/2-inch lengths.
3. Chop the onion fairly fine.
4. Distribute wieners over the bottom of the baking dish.
5. Spoon beans over wieners. There is not enough to cover the wieners, but don't worry about this. Do not use a smaller pan or more beans, just spoon them on as best you can.
6. Sprinkle onion on top of beans.
7. Sprinkle grated cheese on top of onion.
8. Crush the chips. (Just scrunch them up with your fingers before opening the package.) Sprinkle broken chips over the cheese.
9. Pour the taco sauce over all. Don't use a larger size jar or the chips will become too soggy.
10. Bake for 45 minutes.

Serves 4 to 5.

Note: This does not freeze well. You may, however, make the dish ahead, the night before or in the morning, but don't put the chips and taco sauce on until just before you place it in the oven.

Variation

If you don't want this dish to be quite so hot, try substituting canned spaghetti sauce for the taco sauce.

Busy Day Ham Wellington

Great to serve as company fare or homestyle. Because the ham is enclosed in a biscuit dough, the flavors really penetrate. Also excellent served cold the following day.

1 canned ham
¼ cup liquid honey
¼ teaspoon ground cloves
¼ teaspoon dry mustard
   powder
1 package Pillsbury Crescent
   Rolls

Utensils needed:
can opener
small bowl
cookie sheet

1. Heat oven to 375 degrees.
2. Open the can of ham and drain liquid from it.
3. Dry ham thoroughly by patting with paper towels.
4. Mix honey, cloves, and mustard powder together in a small bowl.
5. Open the crescent rolls according to package instructions.
6. Do not separate the dough triangles, but lay the sheet of dough out on a counter and push together along perforation marks to make a solid rectangle of dough.
7. Set ham on dough and spread entire surface with honey mixture.
8. Fold sides of dough up over ham, pressing edges together, then turn the package over (so seam is facing down) to place on a baking sheet. Tuck dough under at both ends.
9. Bake in a 375-degree oven for 30 minutes. Crust will be golden brown.
10. To serve, transfer to a platter (use two spatulas) and cut into 1-inch slices.

Serves 6.

Suggested Accompaniments: Baked acorn squash (cut squash in half, scoop out the seeds, sprinkle cavity with salt and pepper, and top with a dab of butter, then bake at 350 degrees for 1 hour), Green Beans, Cole Slaw.

Broiled Honey'd Ham Steak

¼ cup orange marmalade
2 tablespoons liquid honey
1 center-cut ham steak, about
   1 inch thick
8 whole cloves

Utensils needed:
small bowl
small broiler pan*

1. Turn broiler on.
2. In a small bowl, stir together the marmalade and honey until well mixed. Set aside.
3. Score the outside fat of the ham by cutting through the fat at about 1-inch intervals, *almost* to the meat. This prevents it from curling. Stud the fat with cloves.
4. Place the ham steak on the broiler pan. With oven door open, broil about 3 to 4 inches from heat for 3 minutes on the first side. Turn ham over and spread uncooked side with the marmalade-honey mixture.
5. Broil the second side for 5 to 6 minutes or until it looks dark golden brown around the edges.

Serves 2 to 3.

Suggested Accompaniments: Baked Potato, creamed corn, Green Beans.

* If you have no small broiler pan, place a small wire trivet or cake cooler rack on a cookie sheet. If you spread foil on the pan first, it makes cleaning up a little easier.

Broiled Lamb Chops

Remember: When broiling, oven door is always left open. (Line the broiler pan with foil for easy cleaning.)

4 *loin* lamb chops, 1 inch
   thick
garlic salt
pepper

Utensils needed:
broiler pan

1. Turn broiler on.
2. Place chops on the broiler pan and, when broiler has been on for at least 5 minutes, place broiler pan on top rung in open oven and broil chops until brown, about 5 minutes. *Then* sprinkle the cooked side with garlic salt and pepper.
3. Turn and broil the uncooked side for an additional 5 to 6 minutes. Sprinkle with garlic salt and pepper.

Serves 2.

Note: You want the chops slightly pink around the bone. Thicker chops will require a longer cooking time — 1 or 2 minutes more each side.

Variation

For *shoulder* lamb chops, cook exactly as for loin chops but marinate first in the following marinade.

1 large clove garlic
½ cup oil
1 tablespoon white wine
⅛ teaspoon crushed
   rosemary

1. Mince the garlic.
2. Combine all ingredients and pour over shoulder lamb chops in a shallow bowl. Let chops sit for 2 hours or more, turning once or twice during this time.
3. Remove from marinade and follow cooking instructions for loin chops.

Serves 2.

Suggested Accompaniments: Potatoes (baked or French-fried), green peas, Cauliflower with Cheese Sauce or Broiled Tomato Halves, mint jelly.

Baked Lamb Chops

If you have not yet christened your broiler and don't feel like experimenting with expensive lamb chops, you can bake them.

2 *loin* lamb chops*
Worcestershire sauce
  (roughly 1 teaspoon
  per chop)
fresh lemon juice (roughly
  1 teaspoon per chop)
1 teaspoon butter per chop

Utensils needed:
2-tined fork
small, shallow baking pan

1. Poke holes all over lamb chops, then sprinkle with both the Worcestershire sauce and lemon juice. Top with butter.
2. Bake in a preheated 375 degree oven for 15 to 20 minutes. The meat will be pink, which is exactly how most lamb-lovers prefer it, for maximum texture and flavor. If you prefer your lamb well-done, increase the cooking time to 30 to 35 minutes.

Serves 1 or 2.

Suggested accompaniments: Baked sweet potatoes and green peas.

* You might need two chops per person, depending on the size.

Liver with Onions & Bacon

If you have been brought up to believe you should eat liver once a week, you must know how to cook it. Liver-lovers are fairly well split between those who insist it should be served with onions and those who feel it is best when served with bacon. This sauce will satisfy both.

1 pound calf's liver
4 slices bacon
3 tablespoons all-purpose
   flour
1 can onion soup (10 oz.)
4 tablespoons chili sauce
(no salt)

Utensils needed:
electric fry pan or large fry
   pan with lid
can opener
small bowl

1. Remove the thin outer skin from sliced liver. (Most liver purchased at the supermarket comes already sliced and most butchers slice it about 1/3 inch thick.)
2. Turn electric fry pan to about 325 degrees and fry bacon until crisp. If you are doing this in a non-electric fry pan, place pan over medium heat to cook the bacon.
3. When bacon is cooked, remove to paper towels and pour off half the bacon fat from the pan.
4. Sprinkle flour on a piece of wax paper or plastic wrap; dip liver slices one by one in the flour, turning to coat both sides.
5. Cook liver in bacon fat in the fry pan over medium heat, about 2 to 3 minutes on each side, just enough to brown lightly. Liver toughens when it is overcooked, so don't overdo it.
6. Combine undiluted soup with the chili sauce in a small bowl. Tear bacon into 1-inch pieces and add to sauce.
7. Pour sauce over liver. Cover the fry pan, turn heat to low, and simmer the liver and sauce for 5 minutes.
8. Remove cover and simmer for an additional 5 minutes, just long enough to thicken sauce a bit.
9. Serve hot.

Serves 4.

Suggested Accompaniments: Mashed Potatoes, Green Beans, corn.

Main Dishes
Poultry

Roast Chicken
Poultry Stuffing
Giblet Gravy
Roast Turkey
Easy Company Chicken
Herb-Baked Chicken
Chicken Wellington
Baked Chicken Pieces
Chicken Stir-Fry
Taco Drumsticks
Busy Day Chicken
Swiss-Baked Chicken Breasts
Garnet's Breasts

Helpful Hint

If you have no string for tying your chicken or turkey before
roasting, use dental floss. It is very strong and doesn't burn.

Roast Chicken

4- to 5-pound roasting
  chicken
2 tablespoons oil
¼ teaspoon salt
¼ teaspoon pepper
¼ teaspoon thyme
¼ teaspoon sage

Utensils needed:
roasting pan or large baking
  dish, with rack

1. Heat oven to 375 degrees.
2. Remove giblets from the chicken and reserve. (In the chickens you buy in the supermarket, the giblets have been placed in a small paper bag, stuffed inside the chicken.)
3. Run chicken under cold water and pat dry with paper towels, inside and out.
4. At this point either stuff dressing (recipe follows) into the body cavity or simply stuff with an onion cut in half.
5. Pour oil into a corner of the roaster, then, with your fingers, mix in the seasonings.
6. Transfer the chicken to the roaster and rub the oil-and-seasoning mixture all over the outside skin of the bird.
7. If you have stuffed the chicken, close the cavity by sewing together with a needle and thread (or you can use skewers). Draw the legs and wings close to the body and secure with string.
8. Place chicken, breast side up, on a rack in the roasting pan.
9. Bake uncovered in the oven at 375 degrees for 1½ to 2 hours, if unstuffed. If stuffed, cook for 2 to 2½ hours.
10. Spoon the juice that accumulates in the pan over the chicken every 15 minutes during the last hour of cooking.
11. Chicken is done when, if you prick the meat near the thigh joint with a fork, the juices run clear yellow, with no trace of pink. You should also be able to wiggle the leg bone freely. If you use a meat thermometer, insert it in the thickest part of the thigh, not touching a bone; chicken is done when it registers 185 degrees.
12. Transfer bird to a platter. Remove string and thread or skewers. Let stand 10 minutes for easier carving.

Serves 5 to 6.

Suggested Accompaniments: Mashed Potatoes, Brussels Sprouts or peas, baked acorn squash.

Poultry Stuffing (or Dressing)

Always allow about ¾ cup for each pound of poultry. The quantities here make enough stuffing for a 5-pound chicken.

1 large onion
½ cup butter or
  margarine
½ teaspoon salt
½ teaspoon sage
½ teaspoon thyme
¼ teaspoon pepper
2 tablespoons chopped
  parsley
¾ cup chopped celery
5 cups bread crumbs

Utensils needed:
fry pan
J-cloth (or net stuffing bag —
  see page 116)

1. Chop the onion coarsely.
2. Melt the butter in the fry pan, then add onion, spices, herbs, and celery. Fry gently over medium heat, stirring constantly.
3. When onions have turned golden, remove pan from heat and add bread crumbs.
4. Blend well.
5. *To stuff the chicken:* Line the inside of the chicken cavity with a damp J-cloth that you have unfolded to a single thickness. Spoon dressing into the lined cavity. Pull the ends of the J-cloth together and tie, forming a bag.
6. When the chicken is cooked, it will be easy simply to pull the J-cloth bag out and empty dressing into a bowl to serve. (Don't try to use the J-cloth method on small frying chickens because the cavity is too small.)

Note: Stuffing may be made up to a day in advance, but never stuff the bird prior to roasting time. It is also not advisable to store leftover dressing in poultry when it is cooked, so the J-cloth bag method serves two purposes.

Giblet Gravy

For a supermarket chicken, the giblets are found in a paper bag, generally in the neck cavity of the chicken or turkey along with the heart and liver. Use only the giblets and heart. Feed the liver to the cat or your friend's cat.

giblets from 1 chicken
water
2 tablespoons all-purpose
   flour
salt and pepper

Utensils needed:
small saucepan
large measuring cup
wooden spoon

1. While chicken is roasting, place giblets and heart in a saucepan. Add enough cold water to cover, and bring to a boil over high heat. Cover saucepan and reduce heat to low.
2. Simmer until giblets are tender when pierced with a fork, at least an hour.
3. Remove from heat, drain, and reserve broth for gravy.
4. Chop giblets finely. Discard the heart.
5. When the chicken is cooked, remove it to a serving platter. You will prepare the gravy in the roasting pan.
6. Add 1 cup of reserved giblet liquid to the pan drippings. Place the pan over medium heat and scrape browned particles free from the bottom. Pour mixture into a large measuring cup. The fat will rise to the top.
7. Spoon the fat off the mixture in the measuring cup, and measure 2 tablespoons of fat into the roasting pan. If you need more fat, use butter.
8. Add enough giblet juice to the drippings remaining in the measuring cup to make 1 cup.
9. Heat fat over medium heat. Stir in the flour with a wooden spoon and cook until bubbly. Remove from heat and gradually stir in the giblet stock mixture from the measuring cup. Stir constantly until gravy boils and thickens.
10. Stir in the chopped giblets and season with salt and pepper to taste.

Note: These quantities make 1 cup of gravy. If you wish to make more, use 2 tablespoons fat and 2 tablespoons all-purpose flour for each cup of liquid.

Roast Turkey

Prepare the bird exactly as for Roast Chicken (page 113).

Use the stuffing recipe on page 114, but note you will need 3/4 cup stuffing for each pound of poultry. If you are cooking a large bird — over 8 pounds — increase the ingredients proportionately.

The J-cloth method described on page 114 (to stuff a chicken) works well on smaller turkeys — up to about 10 pounds. For larger turkeys, see the note below.

There is nothing wrong with the packaged stuffing mixes. Simply follow package directions. You might add a can of drained sliced mushrooms or, if it is a large turkey, water chestnuts cut in large dice.

We prefer to cook turkeys at a lower temperature than chickens. The following timetable is a good guide for cooking stuffed turkey at an oven temperature of 325 degrees.

Pounds	Time
6-8	3¾-4 hours
8-10	4-4½
10-12	4½-5
12-14	5-5½
14-16	5½-6
16-18	6-6½
18-20	6½-7½
20-24	7½-9

If you plan to cook the turkey unstuffed, allow 5 minutes per pound *less* cooking time.

Note: A turkey stuffing bag is an invaluable item to have on hand when dressing a large bird. The stuffing is placed inside the bag, which is tied with string and placed in the turkey cavity. When the turkey is cooked, simply remove the bag and empty stuffing into a serving dish. It is not advisable to leave any stuffing inside poultry after it is cooked; this method removes the stuffing entirely.

To make a stuffing bag you will need about half a yard of 45-inch-wide netting. Cut into six rectangles of 9" x 15". Fold each rectangle in half along the longest edge and sew up two sides. You now have several inexpensive bags for your use. They are washable and make a dandy gift!

Easy Company Chicken

Hard to believe anything this simple to prepare can be company fare, but don't tell them and they'll never guess.

12 chicken pieces
(breasts, thighs,
or assorted)
salt
garlic powder
1 bottle Russian dressing
(8 oz.)
2 packages dry onion soup
mix
1 jar apricot jam
(9 oz.)
½ cup water

Utensils needed:
large baking dish
medium bowl

1. Heat the oven to 350 degrees. Grease the baking dish.
2. Wash the chicken pieces. Dry on paper towels and place in a single layer in the greased casserole.
3. Sprinkle with salt and garlic powder.
4. Mix all other ingredients together in a bowl, then pour over the chicken pieces. Cover the baking dish with a lid or aluminum foil.
5. Bake for 1¼ to 1¾ hours.
6. Uncover and bake for 15 minutes more.

Serves 6 to 8.

Note: This makes quite a large amount of sauce, so you won't need to increase the recipe if you use more chicken.

Suggested Accompaniments: Hot Fluffy Rice, green peas or Green Beans, Tossed Green Salad.

Herb-Baked Chicken

If you are really pressed for time, this recipe will be invaluable. Any leftover portion is nice cold the next day.

2½ to 3 pounds cut-up
   chicken
⅓ cup melted butter
salt and pepper
sweet basil
thyme

Utensils needed:
shallow baking dish

1. Turn oven to 400 degrees.
2. Brush chicken with melted butter on both sides and place *skin side down* in a shallow baking dish in a single layer.
3. Sprinkle with salt, pepper, sweet basil, and thyme.
4. Bake uncovered at 400 degrees for 30 minutes.
5. Turn *skin side up,* sprinkle with additional salt, pepper, sweet basil, and thyme, and bake for a further 30 minutes. The skin will crisp up nicely and have a delightful flavor.

Serves 4.

Suggested Accompaniments: Rice or Baked Potato, Green Beans or peas, Tossed Green Salad.

Chicken Wellington

1 package frozen puff pastry,
   defrosted (1 lb.)
1 package cream cheese,
   room temperature (4 oz.)
2 whole chicken breasts
2 tablespoons butter
salt and pepper
⅛ teaspoon garlic powder
2 tablespoons chopped
   parsley

Utensils needed:
sharp knife
small fry pan
small bowl
rolling pin
cookie sheet

1. Make sure the puff pastry is thawed and the cream cheese has been left out at room temperature for a while.
2. Turn oven to 425 degrees.
3. Peel off the skin from the chicken breasts. Cut cleanly along the center of the breastbone with a very sharp knife and, sliding the knife across the bone the whole way, cut meat away from bone. (For a more detailed description of how to bone chicken breast, see page 125.) You will now have 4 pieces of boneless, skinless chicken.
4. Melt butter in a small skillet over medium heat and fry chicken breasts gently for 2 to 3 minutes on each side. Chicken should be cooked through by this time. Sprinkle lightly with salt and pepper as they are cooking.
5. Remove chicken from fry pan and let cool to room temperature while you prepare the remaining ingredients.
6. Combine cream cheese, garlic powder, and parsley in a small bowl. A mixer is handy for this but not necessary. Mix until smooth and creamy.
7. Roll out pastry according to directions on package and cut into 4 8- by 6-inch rectangles.
8. Divide cream cheese mixture in 4 and spread one portion of mixture lengthwise down the middle of each rectangle of pastry. Place chicken breasts on top of this.
9. Moisten edges of pastry with water, bring pastry up over chicken, and pinch edges together to seal. Place seam side down on the ungreased cookie sheet.
10. Bake for 25 minutes or until pastry is golden brown.

Serves 3 to 4.

Suggested Accompaniments: Glazed Carrots, package of frozen spinach soufflé (follow directions on package).

Baked Chicken Pieces

For when you really have no time or inclination to fuss. It is tasty enough to serve at a party, too.

2½ to 3 pounds cut-up
  chicken
1 package dehydrated onion
  soup mix (1.5 oz.)
1½ tablespoons butter

Utensils needed:
large shallow baking dish

1. Turn oven to 350 degrees.
2. Place chicken pieces in a single layer in a shallow baking pan.
3. Sprinkle chicken with dry onion soup mix and dot with butter.
4. Cover chicken with foil and bake in oven at 350 degrees for 1 hour.

Serves 4.

Suggested Accompaniments: Hot Fluffy Rice (spoon some of the sauce from the baking pan over the rice), Tossed Green Salad.

Chicken Stir-Fry

Simple to prepare, eye-appealing, and lo-cal to boot.

2 tablespoons fresh lemon
  juice
2 tablespoons vegetable oil
pinch of ginger or
  ¼ teaspoon grated
  fresh ginger*
½ pound boneless chicken
  breast, cut in long strips
3 green onions, cut in 1½"
  lengths
1 small green pepper, cut in
  long strips (discard seeds)

Utensils needed:
medium bowl
small bowl (or cup)
large frying pan or wok
grater

1 small red pepper (sweet),
  cut in long strips (discard
  seeds)
¼ pound pea pods
8 fresh mushrooms, cut in
  quarters
3 tablespoons cold water
1 tablespoon cornstarch
½ teaspoon sugar
2 tablespoons white wine
¼ cup cashews, optional

1. Combine lemon juice, oil, and ginger in a medium-size bowl.
2. Add chicken strips; stir to coat and let sit for 30 minutes to
   1 hour to marinate.
3. Clean vegetables and cut up as specified above.
4. Place the water in a cup or small bowl; stir in cornstarch, then
   sugar, then wine. Set aside until needed during the final stage
   of cooking.
5. Place a large frying pan or wok over high heat and add
   chicken, plus marinade. Stir constantly with a wooden spoon
   until chicken changes color (it will turn whitish); this will take
   only 2 to 3 minutes.
6. As soon as chicken looks cooked, stir in the green and red
   peppers, green onions, and pea pods. Continue to cook
   over high heat, stirring most of the time, for an additional
   3 minutes.
7. Stir in the mushrooms (these don't take as long). Cook for
   another minute or two.
8. With your wooden spoon, push vegetables and chicken to
   sides of pan and pour the cornstarch-water mixture into
   center of pan. Cook, stirring this liquid constantly until it boils
   and thickens. (If you use cashews, add now.)
9. Stir vegetables around in this mixture until coated. (Avoid
   overcooking the vegetables, as tender-crisp and colorful
   vegetables are the sign of a good stir-fry!)

Serves 2 to 4.

Suggested Accompaniments: Boiled rice, or *our* favorite:
served over cooked fettucine noodles.

* The flavor of this dish is improved considerably by using the fresh
ginger root rather than the powdered ginger.
(If you don't know what it looks like, ask your produce manager.)
Peel a small piece and grate it onto a piece of wax paper or plastic
wrap. Measure out 1/4 teaspoon and add it to the marinade.

Taco Drumsticks

2 eggs
1 package taco-flavored
   tortilla chips (9 oz.)
2 to 3 pounds chicken
   drumsticks
1 can pizza sauce
   (7½ oz.)

Utensils needed:
small bowl
small plastic or paper bag
shallow baking dish or
   cookie sheet
can opener
small saucepan

1. Turn oven to 350 degrees.
2. Beat the eggs slightly in a small bowl.
3. Crush the tortilla chips fairly fine and place the crumbs in a small plastic or paper bag.
4. Dip the chicken drumsticks one at a time in the egg, then shake one at a time in the tortilla crumbs to coat.
5. Arrange in a shallow baking pan and bake for 55 to 60 minutes.
6. Heat the pizza sauce in a saucepan, pour into a small serving bowl, and serve as a side dish in which to dip the chicken.

Serves 3 to 4.

Suggested Accompaniments: Baked Potatoes or rice, corn, Cole Slaw.

Busy Day Chicken

This dish was designed for those days when your horoscope advises to take it easy. It is a complete meal and prepared quickly and easily.

2 medium onions
2 medium potatoes
3 medium carrots
1 tablespoon butter
2 tablespoons oil
2½ to 3 pounds cut-up
   chicken
2 teaspoons garlic powder
2 teaspoons oregano
1 cup water
salt and pepper

Utensils needed:
vegetable peeler
electric fry pan or
   Dutch oven
spatula

1. Chop the onions, and pare and quarter the potatoes and carrots.
2. Place butter and oil in a fry pan or Dutch oven, then turn heat to medium.
3. Add onion and cook until onions are soft — about 5 minutes.
4. Push onions aside a bit and add chicken pieces. Sprinkle with 1 teaspoon of garlic powder and 1 teaspoon oregano and brown slightly, for about 5 minutes. Turn chicken over and sprinkle with remaining garlic powder and oregano. Brown this side slightly for an additional 4 minutes.
5. Add potatoes, carrots, and water. Sprinkle with salt and pepper. Place lid on and turn heat to high, just long enough until water starts to boil (you will hear it and see the steam). Turn heat to low and simmer for 35 minutes.

Serves 3 to 4.

Swiss-Baked Chicken Breasts

If you like chicken, cheese, and mushrooms and if you like simple dishes, we recommend the following.

2 whole chicken breasts
salt and pepper
8 fresh mushrooms
2 tablespoons chopped fresh parsley
4 slices Swiss cheese
4 slices mozzarella cheese

Utensils needed:
9″ square, shallow baking dish

1. Turn oven to 350 degrees.
2. Bone and skin the breasts (see next recipe, or you can buy breasts already boned). You should now have 4 pieces of skinless, boneless chicken.
3. Sprinkle the chicken pieces lightly with salt and pepper and place in a shallow baking dish in a single layer.
4. Wipe the mushrooms. Slice them over the chicken, then sprinkle with parsley.
5. Top each piece of chicken with a slice of Swiss cheese, then a slice of mozzarella cheese.
6. Bake for 40 to 45 minutes.

Serves 3 to 4.

Suggested Accompaniments: Hot Fluffy Rice, French-style green beans, Tossed Green Salad.

Garnet's Breasts

Simple yet elegant. If you are counting calories, omit the cream and it will still be excellent.

2 whole chicken breasts
½ cup bread crumbs*
¼ cup wheat germ
¼ teaspoon thyme
2 tablespoons oil
2 tablespoons butter
½ cup sherry
¼ cup whipping cream

Utensils needed:
shallow bowl
large fry pan
9″ square, shallow
  baking dish

1. Bone and skin the breasts. (See note opposite. You can buy breasts already boned, but with a pair of kitchen shears and a sharp knife, it is a simple procedure and not so costly.)
2. Mix bread crumbs, wheat germ, and thyme in a shallow bowl.
3. Firmly press each chicken piece into this mixture to coat both sides.
4. Refrigerate until ready to cook. Chicken should sit in the refrigerator for at least 15 minutes to set the crumbs so they will adhere better during frying.
5. When you are ready to cook the breasts, turn oven to 350 degrees.
6. Heat oil and butter in the fry pan over medium heat. When butter starts to sizzle, add chicken pieces and lightly brown on both sides. This will take about 3 to 4 minutes on each side.
7. Transfer to a baking dish in a single layer.
8. Add sherry to the fry pan and boil briskly until reduced by half, scraping up brown bits stuck to bottom. Reduce heat, add cream, and simmer for 2 minutes, stirring constantly. (Do not use cereal cream — half and half; it will curdle.)
9. Pour sherry sauce over breasts. Bake in preheated oven for 20 minutes. The breasts don't need to bake too long because they are mostly cooked from the frying.

Serves 3 to 4.

* Use day-old bread for the crumbs instead of buying the dry packaged bread crumbs.

Note: To bone a chicken breast, place the whole breast skin side down. Locate the wishbone, which will be in the center of the thickest part of the breast, right at the front. With sharp shears, cut breast lengthwise in half, through the bone. Insert a sharp knife under the first rib in the rib cage and, with a scraping motion, separate the meat from the bone, working toward the thickest part.

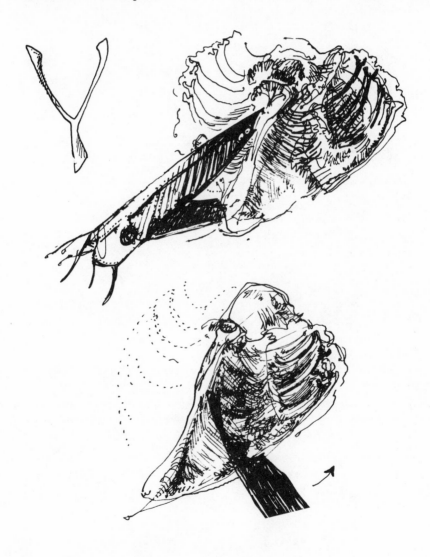

Suggested Accompaniments: Fine boiled noodles (follow instructions on package), Broiled or Baked Zucchini, fresh tomato slices sprinkled with your favorite salad dressing, and lots of chopped fresh parsley.

Main Dishes
Seafood

David Shaw 1983

Broiled Fish Steaks
Fried Fish Fillets
Fish Cakes
Canadian Salmon (Fillets or Steaks)
Shrimp — Boiled
Shrimp — Broiled or Fried
Curried Shrimp
Overnight Crab Casserole
Fillet of Sole
Sole Florentine
Linguine with Crab Sauce
Fettucine Alfredo
Tuna-Potato Chip Casserole

Helpful Hints

1. Fish is often ruined by using too high a heat and cooking for too
   long a period. Overcooked fish is tasteless and dry.

2. Fresh fish should be kept very cold and used as soon as possible.

3. To improve canned shrimp, soak them in ice water for 1 hour
   before using.

4. Add some chopped capers and a bit of lemon juice to
   mayonnaise for a tangy accompaniment to fish.

Broiled Fish Steaks

Most beginners would probably be reluctant to tackle a whole fish, so in this section we haven't included any of those. Instead, we will suggest ways of preparing a few uncomplicated fish dishes you may want to serve to those friends who you know prefer fish to meat (*i.e.,* joggers, health nuts, and that ilk), plus one or two easy supper dishes for *you*. The most important thing to know about fish is the "nose test" — if you can smell it, it isn't fresh!

½ pound fish steak — salmon, halibut, or swordfish
1 tablespoon melted butter
salt and pepper

Utensils needed:
small baking dish

1. Turn broiler on about 10 minutes before cooking and arrange the oven rack so fish will be about 3 to 4 inches from the heat.
2. Brush steaks on *both* sides with the melted butter and salt and pepper. Place in a baking dish.
3. Broil (leaving oven door open) for 3 minutes on one side. Turn steak over and brush with additional butter on uncooked side; broil for an additional 3 minutes. *Do not overcook.* Fish steak is done when it flakes easily with a fork.

Serves 1.

Suggested Accompaniments: Small boiled new potatoes or rice, spinach, broiled tomato halves (sprinkle with garlic salt and black pepper, dot with butter, and broil for 5 minutes), crusty French rolls.

Fried Fish Fillets

½ pound fish fillets — sole,
   haddock, bluefish, cod,
   perch
1 egg
½ cup cracker crumbs
1 tablespoon oil
1 tablespoon butter
salt and pepper

Utensils needed:
shallow bowl
wax paper or plastic wrap
medium fry pan
spatula

1. Wash the fish and dry *thoroughly.*
2. Beat the egg in a shallow bowl. Spread crumbs on a piece of wax paper or plastic wrap.
3. Dip fish in beaten egg, then "roll" in cracker crumbs.
4. Heat oil and butter in the fry pan (heavy pan is best) over moderate to high heat until butter starts to bubble but not burn. Add fish and fry 3 minutes on the first side. Sprinkle with salt and pepper, turn with a spatula, and fry for an additional 3 minutes on the other side, or until fish is golden brown and flakes easily with a fork.
5. Serve at once with lemon wedges or tartar sauce.*

Serves 2.

Variations

This method may be used on scallops or oysters as well.

Small whole fish such as smelt or trout should be rolled in cornmeal rather than cracker crumbs and cooked as above.

Suggested Accompaniments: Hot Fluffy Rice, Tossed Green Salad.

*Easy Tartar Sauce

Stir 2 tablespoons sweet pickle relish (the kind you put on hot dogs, but not the mustard type) into ½ cup mayonnaise. (Tartar sauce is also available ready-made at the supermarket.)

Fish Cakes

This makes a good supper dish and is a splendid way of using up leftover cooked fish. It is convenient if you just happen to have leftover mashed potatoes as well, but if not, the instant kind will do.

1 cup cooked fish
2 cups mashed potatoes*
1 beaten egg
½ teaspoon salt
⅛ teaspoon pepper
2 tablespoons chopped fresh
  parsley — optional
¼ cup all-purpose flour
2 tablespoons oil

Utensils needed:
large bowl
fry pan
spatula

1. Mash fish and potatoes together with the egg in a large bowl. Season with salt and pepper and add parsley.
2. With your hands, shape the fish mixture into cakes about 2½ inches in diameter and ½ inch thick.
3. Spread flour on a plate or piece of wax paper.
4. Dip both sides of cakes in the flour.
5. Heat the oil in the fry pan and fry fish cakes on both sides until golden brown, about 2 to 3 minutes on each side.

Serves 2.

Variation

Instead of cooked fish, you may use canned salmon (the cheapest brand, pink, is fine).

Suggested Accompaniments: Peas, Tossed Green Salad.

* Can use instant; follow directions on package.

Canadian Salmon (Fillets or Steaks)

Not that this method wouldn't work equally well on salmon caught off the coast of the U.S., but the recipe came to us via Jalna Patey, wife of British Columbian commercial fisherman, via Edmontonian Bill Tuele. The amounts of topping will vary depending on the size of the fish you are cooking, so use your judgment. You also need to use a bit of common sense when it comes to timing. For instance, a fish straight from the refrigerator will take a few minutes longer than when it has been sitting on a counter in a warm kitchen for an hour. *Fish is cooked when it is opaque through its thickest part.*

Fillet of Salmon

whole fillet of salmon*　　　Utensils needed:
mayonnaise　　　　　　　　large, flat baking pan
brown sugar　　　　　　　　pair of tweezers
soy sauce

1. Turn oven to 375 degrees.
2. Place fish fillet, skin-side-down, in a greased, large flat baking pan.
3. Smear the cut surface of the fish with mayonnaise in a thin layer.
4. Sprinkle brown sugar over the mayonnaise, also in a thin layer.
5. Sprinkle soy sauce over the brown sugar — enough to moisten the sugar well.
6. Place fish in the oven and bake for 8 minutes.
7. Turn broiler on, transfer fish to top rack in the oven, and finish cooking under the broiler for 3 minutes.

Servings: It is a good rule of thumb to allow about 1/4 pound of *boneless* fish per person.

* Any butcher will fillet the salmon for you, but he may leave a few of the small bones. Rub your hand over the flesh of the fish (against the grain) and remove any stragglers with a pair of tweezers.

Note: This is also terrific on the barbecue, if you have the hooded type. It will take 11 minutes. The fish will be wonderfully moist and flavorful. Most people tend to overcook fish, which is a big mistake.

Salmon Steaks

You don't get the same "sealing off" of the flesh (skin on the bottom and mayonnaise, etc., on top), but it is still a nice way to cook this particular cut of fish. Steaks are usually cut 1″ thick. They vary in width according to the size of the fish, but the following amounts are sufficient for steaks measuring 3″ in width (not depth).

1 salmon steak
1 tablespoon mayonnaise
2 teaspoons brown sugar
2 teaspoons soy sauce

Utensils needed:
small, flat baking pan

1. Cook as above, but reduce the timing to 5 minutes in a preheated, 375 degree oven; then turn the broiler on and transfer the fish to the top rack for a further 3 minutes under the broiler. (Adjust your racks before you turn the oven on.)

Serves 1.

Shrimp — Boiled

Most people, and not just beginners, tend to overcook shrimp. Don't overcook *any* fish. Remember, fish cooks very quickly, and shrimp are no exception. Cooking shrimp in their shells gives them a better shape; they curl up too much if you shell them first.

water
salt
peppercorns
shrimp

Utensils needed:
large saucepan

1. Bring water to a boil, making sure you have enough water to cover the shrimp well.
2. Add salt, using 1 tablespoon for every quart of water, and peppercorns — 4 should be enough.
3. Add shrimp to boiling water, turn heat down so water is just simmering, and then cover the pot. Cook for 3 minutes — no longer. Shrimp will be pink and tender at this point.
4. Drain immediately and chill.
5. Remove shells and the black vein (the intestine, harmless but unsightly).

Shrimp — Broiled or Fried

The simplest preparations are usually the best when it comes to seafood.

1 pound shrimp
2 cloves garlic
2 tablespoons lemon juice
2 tablespoons finely chopped
  parsley
⅓ cup oil*
salt

Utensils needed:
large bowl
large fry pan or shallow
  baking dish

1. Peel and de-vein the shrimp.
2. Mince the garlic, or chop very small, and combine with all the other ingredients, except shrimp, in a large bowl. Mix well.
3. Add shrimp and stir gently until shrimp are completely coated. You may cover with foil at this point and refrigerate until ready to serve. The actual cooking time will require no more than 6 minutes.
4. **To Fry:** Arrange shrimp in a single layer in a fry pan and pour over them any oil mixture remaining in the bowl. Cook over high heat for 4 minutes, turning once. Sprinkle lightly with salt and cook for 1 additional minute.

   To Broil: Turn broiler on at least 5 minutes before cooking the shrimp. When broiler is ready, place marinated shrimp in a single layer in a shallow pan and broil about 3 to 4 inches from heat for 2 to 3 minutes on each side. (Remember, always leave the oven door open when broiling.) Sprinkle lightly with salt.

Serves 4.

Suggested Accompaniments: Tossed Green Salad, sliced tomatoes, Uncle Ben's Long Grain and Wild Rice mix, crusty French loaf.

* Use olive oil if you have it, otherwise any vegetable oil.

Curried Shrimp

If you feel like going native, add more curry powder.

1 pound shrimp, uncooked
½ medium onion
2 tablespoons butter
1 tablespoon all-purpose
  flour
¼ teaspoon salt
pinch of white pepper
1½ teaspoons curry powder
⅛ teaspoon ginger
1 teaspoon sugar
2 tablespoons sherry
1 to 1½ cups milk

Utensils needed:
large fry pan
wooden spoon

1. Peel and de-vein the shrimp. (If you're using frozen shrimp, they will probably have been prepared. Make sure they are thawed before you cook them.)

2. Chop the onion.

3. Melt butter in the fry pan over medium heat.

4. Gently fry the onion and shrimp in butter until shrimp are cooked — they will turn pink. This will take no longer than 3 minutes.

5. Sprinkle shrimp with flour, salt, pepper, curry powder, ginger, and sugar. Stir until flour has been absorbed.

6. Add sherry and 1 cup milk and stir quickly and constantly until mixture bubbles and thickens. If you prefer a thinner sauce, add a little more milk and return to heat, stirring until mixture just reaches a slow boil. Remove from heat.

7. Serve with hot Fluffy Rice and an assortment of 3 or 4 condiments such as chopped banana, peanuts, raisins, chutney, fresh coconut chips, or chopped fresh peaches.

Serves 3 or 4.

Overnight Crab Casserole

This is great for those busy days when you know you will be getting home late; you make your supper the night before! It is a good idea always to have a couple of hard-boiled eggs in the refrigerator. You will be surprised how often they come in handy. Put an X on the bottom of the hard-boiled ones to identify them easily.

1 can crab (6 oz.)
1 can cream of chicken soup
  (10 oz.)
⅓ cup milk
½ cup Miracle Whip
1½ teaspoons onion flakes*
2 cups extra-fine noodles,
  uncooked
2 hard-boiled eggs
1 cup grated Cheddar cheese

Utensils needed:
grater
can opener
medium bowl
8″ casserole

1. Drain the crab, discarding juice. Empty crabmeat into a mixing bowl and break up slightly with a fork.
2. Stir in undiluted soup, milk, Miracle Whip, and onion flakes.
3. Stir in noodles; don't worry if some of them break.
4. Chop the eggs finely and stir into crab mixture, together with ½ cup of the cheese.
5. Empty into a buttered casserole dish. Top with remaining ½ cup cheese.
6. Refrigerate overnight.
7. At serving time, bake in a preheated 350 degree oven for 30 minutes.

Serves 4.

Suggested Accompaniments: Tossed Green Salad, hot rolls.

* Comes in a small bottle to be found in the spice section of the supermarket.

Fillet of Sole

2 tablespoons butter
¾ cup sliced fresh
  mushrooms
2 tablespoons chopped fresh
  parsley
1 can shrimp soup (10 oz.)
2 tablespoons sherry or dry
  white wine
1 pound sole fillets
paprika

Utensils needed:
small fry pan
can opener
shallow baking dish

1. Turn broiler on.
2. Melt butter in a small fry pan and cook mushrooms slowly until soft, 2 or 3 minutes.
3. Stir in parsley, soup, and sherry; stir until well mixed.
4. Arrange sole in a shallow baking dish and pour soup and mushrooms over it.
5. Place under broiler, about 4 inches from the heat, and broil for 6 minutes, leaving oven door open.
6. Remove from under broiler, sprinkle with paprika, then return to broiler for an additional 2 minutes or until done. Fish is cooked when it flakes easily when tested with a fork. (Paprika burns easily, which is why you do not put it on during the first cooking period.)

Serves 3 to 4.

Note: If you use frozen fillets, dry them well with paper towels before placing in baking dish.

Suggested Accompaniments: Hot Fluffy Rice, buttered spinach, cherry tomatoes.

Sole Florentine

Whenever you see the word *Florentine,* you know there is spinach in the dish. This fish dish is definitely classified as special and you don't *have* to mention you used a store-bought spinach soufflé.

4 slices bacon
1 pound sole fillets
1 package frozen spinach
   soufflé, thawed
¾ cup crushed rice flakes
2 tablespoons melted butter

Utensils needed:
small fry pan
7″ x 12″ or 8″ square, shallow
   baking dish

1. Cook bacon until crisp and set aside. Crumble when cool.
2. Turn oven to 400 degrees. Butter a shallow baking dish.
3. Place sole in the buttered baking dish. (If fish was frozen, dry well with paper towels first, as frozen fish tends to be a bit watery.)
4. Spoon soufflé on top of fillets (don't spread too thinly), leaving about 1 inch of fish showing around the edges.
5. Combine the melted butter and rice flakes and sprinkle all over the top of the dish.
6. Top this with crumbled bacon.
7. Bake at 400 degrees for 15 to 20 minutes, or until cooked. Fish is cooked when it flakes easily when tested with a fork.

Serves 4.

Suggested Accompaniments: Whole cherry tomatoes or broiled tomato halves, Uncle Ben's Long Grain and Wild Rice mix.

Linguine with Crab Sauce

Absolutely delicious and not a calorie, as you can see!

12 ounces linguine
½ cup butter
1 clove garlic
1 cup whipping cream
½ cup grated Parmesan
  cheese
1 can crab, drained (6 oz.)
½ teaspoon salt
¼ teaspoon black pepper*
2 tablespoons chopped fresh
  parsley

Utensils needed:
large saucepan
colander
can opener
large fry pan

1. Cook linguine according to package directions. Drain well in a colander, then transfer to a serving platter.
2. While linguine is cooking, melt the butter in a large fry pan over low heat.
3. Mince the garlic and add to melted butter. Cook until garlic is soft.
4. Add cream and, stirring constantly, let it simmer until it starts to thicken a bit. This will take about 5 minutes.
5. Stir in the Parmesan cheese, drained crab, salt and pepper. Stir over low heat until well heated through, about an additional 2 to 3 minutes.
6. Pour over cooked linguine and toss lightly.
7. Serve topped with chopped fresh parsley.

Serves 4.

Fettucine Alfredo

To transfer the above dish into the classic "Fettucine Alfredo," simply substitute fettucine noodles for the linguine and delete the crab. Have a pepper grinder on hand for those who want a fresh grinding of pepper over top.

Variations

You may substitute spaghetti for linguine. Cook according to directions on the package, but don't overcook. You want spaghetti cooked to the *al dente* (bitey) stage. How can you tell when the linguine or spaghetti is cooked? Remove one strand and throw it against the wall; if it sticks it is done. This is no joke; a lot of people use this method. If you don't fancy picking strands of cooked pasta off the wall, an alternative method is the thumb-and-forefinger test: the cooked strand should be slightly resilient, not mushy, when pressed between thumb and forefinger.

If you prefer to use fresh or frozen crab rather than canned, use 6 to 8 ounces.

Suggested Accompaniments: Tossed Green Salad or Caesar Salad, crusty buns or good-quality French bread; fresh fruit plate for dessert.

* This is one case where freshly ground black pepper really does taste incomparably better than the packaged kind. So if you have a pepper grinder, use it!

Tuna-Potato Chip Casserole

I hate to say this, but if you can't make this, you really are just a born loser in the kitchen.

2 cups coarsely crushed
  potato chips
1 can tuna (6.5 oz.)
1 can cream of mushroom
  soup (10 oz.)
¼ cup milk
2 tablespoons chopped onion
½ cup chopped celery

Utensils needed:
can opener
8″ square baking dish
small bowl

1. Turn oven on to 325 degrees.
2. Sprinkle 1 cup of the crushed potato chips in the bottom of the baking dish.
3. Drain tuna and arrange on top of potato chips.
4. Combine soup with milk, onion, and celery and pour over tuna.
5. Top with remaining crushed potato chips.
6. Bake for 20 minutes.

Serves 4.

Suggested Accompaniment: Tossed Green Salad.

Vegetables

Patio Baked Beans
Broccoli
Stir-Fried Broccoli
Brussels Sprouts
Favorite Way with Cabbage
Carrots
Glazed Carrots
Cauliflower
Creamy Cauliflower
Green Beans (String Beans)
Green Bean Casserole
Sautéed Mushrooms
Barbecued Onions in Foil
Boiled Potatoes
Mashed Potatoes

Day-Before Mashed
  Potatoes
Party Mashed Potatoes
  with Instant Potatoes
Baked Potatoes
Roast Potatoes
Scalloped Potatoes
Quick Potatoes Romanoff
Fluffy Rice
Spanish Rice in Foil
Chinese Snow Pea Pods
Broiled Tomatoes
Baked Tomato Halves
Mashed Turnip
Baked Zucchini

Helpful Hints

1. Vegetables grown below the surface of the soil contain valuable mineral salts in the skins. Scrub the skins rather than peel them, whenever possible.

2. Peeling onions will cause you to shed a tear or two unless you peel them under cold running water. To remove the unpleasant after-odor, rub your hands with vinegar or lemon juice.

3. To remove the skins from tomatoes, put them into boiling water for 1 minute — do only a couple at a time — to loosen the skins, which will then peel off easily. Put peeled tomatoes into the refrigerator to firm them before slicing or chopping.

4. When cooking, vegetables grown below the ground should be started in cold water and vegetables grown above the ground started in boiling water.

5. To keep spaghetti and macaroni from boiling over, put a tablespoon of oil in the water.

Patio Baked Beans

Perfect for a barbecue. It doubles, triples, etc.; make it for six or sixty. If you just happen to be making it for sixty, increase the baking time.

2 cans pork and beans,
   in tomato sauce
   (14 oz. each)
½ cup chopped onion
¼ cup brown sugar
¼ cup chili sauce
2 teaspoons Worcestershire
   sauce
3 slices bacon

Utensils needed:
can opener
2-quart baking dish

1. Turn oven to 300 degrees.
2. Empty beans into the baking dish and pick out the pieces of pork — a dead give-away to doctored-up canned beans!
3. Add all remaining ingredients except bacon and stir until well mixed.
4. Lay the strips of bacon on top. Bake for 1 hour.

Serves 4 to 6.

Broccoli

We find the recipe for stir-frying broccoli (see next page) to be the most popular way of preparing this vegetable, but if you are counting calories you might prefer it boiled or steamed. Broccoli should be soaked in salted water before cooking — 1 teaspoon salt to 1 quart of water — to flush out the little forms of wildlife that sometimes hide in broccoli or cauliflower.

1½ pounds fresh broccoli
water
salt
butter

Utensils needed:
vegetable peeler
4-quart saucepan, or any
    large wide-mouth saucepan
rack (for steaming)

To Boil Broccoli

1. Separate florets from the stem and set aside.
2. Using the vegetable peeler, pare the stalk; then slice into circles, about 1/4 to 1/2 inch thick.
3. To a wide saucepan add about 1 inch of water (place your index finger in the pan and when the water comes up to your first knuckle, that is the right amount). Add 1/4 teaspoon salt to the water and bring water to a boil over high heat.
4. Add prepared broccoli — circles plus florets — to boiling water. Since you've just added cooler ingredients, the water will go off the boil momentarily.
5. When water returns to the boil, turn heat to medium, place a lid on the saucepan, and cook for about 10 minutes.
6. Test with a fork. When the fork enters the broccoli easily it is cooked.
7. Drain immediately and serve topped with a spoonful of butter, which will melt on contact with the hot broccoli.

To Steam Broccoli

1. Follow the instructions above until you reach step 3. Now increase the amount of water to 2 inches. Bring to boil.

2. When water comes to a boil, place prepared broccoli in a steamer or on a rack above the boiling water. Cover and cook for about 15 minutes over high heat.
3. Test and serve as above.

Serves 4.

Variation

To dress up broccoli, serve topped with cheese sauce. This can be made very simply by heating 1 can (10 oz.) Campbell's Cheddar Cheese Soup, undiluted, with 1/2 cup of grated sharp cheese until cheese has melted.

Stir-Fried Broccoli

It is better to undercook broccoli than to overcook it, as with most vegetables.

1 pound fresh broccoli	Utensils needed:
1 clove garlic	vegetable peeler
3 tablespoons oil	wok or fry pan with lid
salt	spatula
black pepper	
1 teaspoon sugar	
½ cup water	

1. Separate florets from the stem and set aside. (You are going to add these later.)
2. Using the vegetable peeler, pare the stalk and then slice diagonally into circles, about 1/4 to 1/2 inch thick. Mince or finely chop the garlic.
3. Heat oil, garlic, and a sprinkling of salt and black pepper in the fry pan or wok and, when hot, add broccoli circles. Fry over fairly high heat for about 2 minutes, stirring constantly.
4. Sprinkle with sugar, add florets and water, and *cover tightly.* Cook for an additional 2 to 3 minutes, or until cooked but still crisp.

Serves 4 to 5.

Brussels Sprouts

When buying Brussels sprouts, look for green-colored, firmly closed ones. Avoid those with wilted leaves or with yellow or black spots.

1 pound Brussels sprouts
2 teaspoons instant chicken
  soup mix
1½ tablespoons butter or
  margarine

Utensils needed:
medium saucepan

1. Cut stems off Brussels sprouts and pull off any wilted outer leaves.
2. Wash thoroughly.
3. Place 1 inch of water in the bottom of a saucepan (that's about a knuckle's depth). Add chicken soup mix and bring to a boil. The chicken mix gives the sprouts a nice flavor, but if you do not have any on hand, substitute 1/2 teaspoon salt.
4. As soon as the water comes to a boil, drop in the Brussels sprouts. Water will go off the boil for a moment.
5. When water returns to bubbling, place a lid on the saucepan and lower heat to medium. Continue cooking for 8 to 10 minutes or until just tender. *Do not overcook.* Test with a fork for doneness.
6. Drain the sprouts and immediately toss with butter.

Serves 4.

Note: If you cut a shallow *X* into the stem end of the sprouts, they will cook more evenly and need a shorter time.

Favorite Way with Cabbage

We will use a whole cabbage in this recipe because it is excellent reheated and, also, it is not possible to buy part of a cabbage! You may add cut-up, uncooked wieners to this recipe just before cooking and then it makes a great meal. Use as many wieners as you like — up to 1 pound.

1 medium onion
1 medium cabbage
2 tablespoons oil
1 tablespoon butter
2 tablespoons instant chicken
  soup mix
salt and pepper

Utensils needed:
Dutch oven or electric
  fry pan

1. Chop the onion finely.
2. Remove wilted outer leaves of cabbage and the hard core at the bottom and discard. Shred remaining cabbage.
3. Heat oil and butter in the Dutch oven or fry pan for 1 minute, then add the onion.
4. Turn heat to medium and cook onion for 1 minute.
5. Turn heat off before adding cabbage.
6. Sprinkle cabbage with the dry soup mix. Cover the pan.
7. Turn heat to high for 1 minute to start things steaming, then turn heat to low and cook for 10 minutes.
8. Remove cover and stir well.
9. Sprinkle lightly with salt and pepper — not too much salt because the chicken soup mix is salty. You may even omit the salt if you are sodium-conscious.
10. Replace cover and turn heat to high again for 1 minute, then back down to low for an additional 10 minutes.
11. Stir again and serve.

Serves 4.

Note: If you use an electric fry pan, don't open the vent on the cover and don't be tempted to add water. You want the ingredients to "steam" together and retain all the goodness of flavor and nutrition. There should be enough moisture in the cabbage for this purpose. If you use a Dutch oven or a large pot that doesn't have a heavy bottom, do add ¼ cup of water, as thinner-bottomed pots have a tendency to burn things (a good thing to know if you haven't purchased all your pots yet).

Carrots

Next to the potato, the carrot is probably the most popular vegetable. Carrots really do help you to see in the dark, at least that is what both our mothers told us, and mothers are very wise.

Utensils needed:
vegetable peeler
small saucepan

Small Young Carrots (late spring-early summer)

1. Scrape with a knife or wash well.
2. Remove ends and place in a saucepan in a small amount of salted water, about ½ teaspoon salt and 1 inch of water.
3. Turn heat to high until water is boiling, then turn heat to medium and continue cooking until carrots are tender when tested with a fork. This will take about 15 minutes, depending on the size of the carrots. You don't want them mushy.
4. Drain immediately. (Never let cooked vegetables sit in water.)
5. Toss with butter — 1 teaspoon or more, to suit your taste.
6. Serve hot.

Mature Carrots (winter)

1. Peel the carrots. (These usually have a tougher skin and require peeling with a vegetable peeler rather than the scraping method used on young carrots.)
2. Cut the peeled carrots into slices or dice, and follow procedure above. If they are thinly sliced, carrots should cook in 10 minutes.

Variations

Hot cooked carrots may also be mashed with a bit of butter and a pinch of either nutmeg or ginger.

If you are in a hurry and have a grating machine or food processor, grated carrots take only 2 minutes to cook. Use only 2 tablespoons of water; as soon as saucepan contents start to "steam" over high heat, turn heat to medium and cook for 2 minutes — no longer.

Glazed Carrots

1 pound carrots
½ teaspoon salt
3 tablespoons butter
½ cup liquid honey

Utensils needed:
vegetable peeler
medium saucepan
medium fry pan

1. Cut ends off carrots, then peel or scrape the carrots. (Use a vegetable peeler for peeling, a sharp knife for scraping.)
2. Cut carrots into 2- to 3-inch pieces.
3. Place carrots in a medium-size saucepan and add water to cover carrots. Add salt.
4. Bring water to a boil over high heat, place a lid on the saucepan, and turn heat to medium.
5. Cook carrots over medium heat until fork-tender. This will take 15 to 20 minutes.
6. While carrots are cooking, combine the butter and honey in a fry pan.
7. When the carrots are cooked, drain off all the water and add carrots to butter and honey in the fry pan. Turn heat to medium. With a spoon, keep turning the carrots in the honey-butter mixture until they are well glazed on all sides.
8. Serve hot.

Serves 4.

Cauliflower

Buy a head of cauliflower that is free of brown spots. You may cook it whole or break it into bite-size florets, whichever you prefer. Always soak cauliflower in salted cold water — about 1 teaspoon salt to 1 quart of water — to remove any "critters" that might be hiding. Do the same with broccoli. Twenty minutes should be sufficient.

1 medium cauliflower
½ teaspoon salt
1 tablespoon butter or
   margarine

Utensils needed:
large saucepan

To Cook Cauliflower Whole

1. Remove outer leaves and cut out the core (the base of the stem).
2. In a saucepan large enough to hold the whole head of cauliflower with enough space at the top to place a lid, place about 1 inch of water. Add salt. Bring water to a boil over high heat.
3. Add the cauliflower and, when water returns to the boil, cover with the lid and turn heat to medium.
4. Cook for 15 to 20 minutes, or until tender when tested with a fork (make sure you test the stem, which will be the last part to cook). Do not overcook, unless you prefer your cauliflower "mushy."
5. Drain immediately and serve topped with the butter. You may sprinkle with chopped parsley or paprika as well.

To Cook Cauliflower Broken into Florets

1. Remove outer leaves and cut out the core. Break cauliflower into bite-size florets and cook as above, reducing cooking time by about one-half.
2. Drain immediately.

Serves 4.

Variation

Cauliflower, too, is delicious served with cheese sauce. (See recipe for easy cheese sauce in the variation for the broccoli recipe on page 147.)

Creamy Cauliflower

1 large head cauliflower
1 carton French Onion Chip
  Dip (8 oz.)
½ cup grated Cheddar
  cheese

Utensils needed:
grater
large saucepan
round baking dish

1. Prepare the cauliflower head as in the preceding recipe, leaving the head whole. Turn oven to 350 degrees.
2. Cook the cauliflower in salted boiling water until tender. Drain.
3. Place cooked cauliflower head in a round baking dish.
4. Cover with the chip dip.
5. Sprinkle with Cheddar cheese.
6. Place in the heated oven for 15 minutes before serving. To make the cheese bubbly and brown, put the baking dish under the broiler for a few minutes before bringing to the table.

Serves 4 to 6.

Green Beans (String Beans)

Frozen green beans, and most certainly canned green beans, cannot compare with fresh. The "French-style" is the best of the frozen variety.

1 pound fresh green beans
¼ teaspoon salt
2 teaspoons butter or margarine

Utensils needed:
medium saucepan

1. Wash green beans and cut off both tips.
2. If the beans are young and fresh, you may want to cook them whole (asparagus-style). If they are more mature, break them into pieces about 1 inch in length. (You can tell whether they are young or mature by the size; the bigger they are, the older they are.)
3. Place roughly 1 inch of water and the 1/4 teaspoon salt in a saucepan and bring to a boil over high heat.
4. Add beans and, when water returns to a boil, cover the pot and turn heat to medium.
5. Cook beans for 10 to 12 minutes, or until fork-tender.
6. Drain immediately and add butter.

Serves 4.

Green Bean Casserole

This dish started appearing on dinner tables shortly after canned French-fried onions first arrived on the scene, about twenty-five years ago, and it is still very popular.

1 package frozen cut green
   beans (1 lb.)
1 can cream of mushroom
   soup (10 oz.)
¼ teaspoon salt
pinch of white pepper
1 can French-fried onions
   (2.8 oz.)

Utensils needed:
medium saucepan
can opener
1½-quart casserole

1. Turn oven to 325 degrees.
2. Cook beans according to directions on package, but don't overcook; cook until just tender.
3. Drain well and rinse briefly in cold water (this helps retain the bright green color).
4. Stir salt and pepper into undiluted soup, then stir in the green beans.
5. Pour mixture into a casserole and sprinkle the top with canned onions.
6. Bake for 20 to 25 minutes or until heated well through.

Serves 4 to 6.

Note: Drained canned green beans work as well in this recipe.

Sautéed Mushrooms

Never wash mushrooms; they absorb moisture in that interesting-looking underside, and it spoils them. Either wipe with a damp cloth or invest in a mushroom brush. If the mushrooms have been sitting around for a few days and have acquired a few dark spots, peel them. They peel very easily.

½ pound mushrooms
3 to 4 tablespoons butter
salt and pepper
1 tablespoon finely chopped
   fresh parsley

Utensils needed:
small or medium fry pan

1. Clean mushrooms and cut off the ends of the stems if they look dark and gritty.
2. Slice the mushrooms, quarter them, or leave them whole, depending on how you prefer them.
3. Melt butter in the fry pan, then add mushrooms.
4. Fry gently (sauté) over medium heat, stirring occasionally, until mushrooms are tender. This will take about 5 minutes.
5. Sprinkle with salt, pepper, and chopped parsley.

Serves 2 to 3.

Barbecued Onions in Foil

2 large onions, preferably
  Spanish
1 cup barbecue sauce (your
  favorite brand)
2 tablespoons butter

Utensils needed:
aluminum foil

1. Heat oven to 375 degrees.
2. Peel the onions, slice, and separate into rings.
3. Dampen a double square of paper towel (by running under the water tap briefly).
4. Lay a sheet of foil 12 to 14 inches long on your kitchen counter, center the damp towel on top, and place another piece of foil of equal length on top. (This procedure ensures that the food won't scorch or burn.)
5. Place onion rings on foil in the center, over the (hidden) damp towel.
6. Pour on barbecue sauce.
7. Dot with small pieces of butter.
8. From opposite sides, bring both thicknesses of foil together over the onions and fold over twice to seal well. Seal each end with a double fold. You have now created a sealed foil "packet."
9. Bake for 20 minutes in the oven at 375 degrees. Don't overbake or onions will become mushy.

Serves 4.

Variation

These may also be cooked on the barbecue and are terrific served with barbecued steak or a roast.

Boiled Potatoes

There is a variation between boiling mature potatoes and boiling new ones, so here are both methods. (It is always a good idea to remove potatoes from the plastic bag they are packaged in. Store them loosely packed in an open container in a cool place.)

Mature Potatoes

6 medium potatoes
  (about 2 lbs.)
4 cups boiling water
¼ teaspoon salt
2 to 3 tablespoons
  melted butter
3 to 4 tablespoons chopped
  fresh parsley
  or chives

Utensils needed:
vegetable peeler
large saucepan

1. Wash potatoes well, remove sprouts and blemishes, then peel.
2. Cut into quarters and place in a saucepan.
3. Cover with boiling water; add salt.
4. Place over high heat until water comes to a full rolling boil, then turn heat to medium, cover, and cook for 20 to 30 minutes.
5. When fork-tender, remove from heat and drain well.
6. Add melted butter and parsley or chives.
7. Transfer to serving dish.

New Potatoes

12 small new potatoes
boiling water to cover
¼ teaspoon salt
3 to 5 tablespoons
  melted butter
3 to 4 tablespoons chopped
  fresh parsley

Utensils needed:
large saucepan

1. Scrub potatoes well. Do not peel.
2. Transfer to the saucepan and cover with boiling water; add salt.

3. Place over high heat until water comes to a full rolling boil, then reduce heat to medium, cover, and cook for 15 to 20 minutes, or until fork-tender.
4. Remove from heat and drain.
5. Add melted butter and parsley.
6. Transfer to serving dish.

Serves 4 to 6.

Note: The new potatoes are best served with their skins on, but if you wish to peel them do it after cooking. A small 2-pronged fork is useful as a holding tool.

Mashed Potatoes

Older (starchier) potatoes are best for mashed potatoes.

6 medium potatoes
4 cups boiling water
¼ teaspoon salt
3 tablespoons butter
1 teaspoon salt
⅓ cup milk or cereal cream
 (half and half)
pepper

Utensils needed:
vegetable peeler
large saucepan
potato masher or
 electric mixer

1. Proceed as for boiled mature potatoes, steps 1 through 5 on page 158.
2. Add butter, salt, and milk to the drained potatoes.
3. Mash vigorously with a potato masher or beat with an electric mixer until smooth and creamy.
4. Add pepper to taste and transfer to serving dish.
5. Serve immediately.

Serves 4 to 6.

Day-Before Mashed Potatoes

If you want to be free to concentrate on the rest of dinner, this method eliminates last-minute preparation of the potatoes. The dish may be made early in the day, or even the day before, and reheated.

3 cups mashed potatoes*
2 eggs, well beaten
½ cup cereal cream
  (half and half)
salt and pepper

Utensils needed:
medium bowl
electric mixer
1½-quart casserole

1. Butter the casserole dish.
2. In a mixing bowl, combine mashed potatoes with the eggs, cream, and salt and pepper to taste.
3. Beat until light and fluffy.
4. Turn into the buttered baking dish.
5. Refrigerate until needed, but remove from refrigerator at least 1 hour before baking.
6. Bake in a preheated oven at 350 degrees for 30 minutes.

Serves 6.

* See preceding recipe.

Party Mashed Potatoes
with Instant Potatoes

An instant success!

Mashed potatoes from scratch can be a hassle for a beginner if he or she has to cope with coordinating an entire meal for guests. We have given a suggestion for "lump-free" gravy (page 82); now here is a guaranteed "lump-free" mashed potato recipe.

1 large clove garlic, minced
3 cups boiling water
  (less 2 tablespoons)
1 teaspoon salt
2 tablespoons butter
1 cup cold milk
3 cups instant mashed
  potatoes
1 large egg, plus 1 yolk
2 good pinches of cayenne
  pepper (about
  1/16 teaspoon)
2/3 cup grated Cheddar
  cheese

Utensils needed:
1-quart casserole dish
  or 8 individual foil
  muffin cups

1. Place freshly minced garlic in bottom of a large mixing bowl. Add boiling water, salt, butter, and cold milk. Stir in potato flakes gently with a fork.
2. Allow to stand for 30 seconds; then, with a fork or wire whisk, whip in the egg, the egg yolk, and cayenne pepper. Spoon mixture into a 1-quart buttered casserole dish and sprinkle top with grated cheese.
3. Bake in a preheated 425-degree oven for 25 to 30 minutes.

Serves 6 to 8.

Note: We have made these for barbecue parties, using the individual foil muffin cups (3¾" x 1⅝"). These are available at most supermarkets. Butter them before you add the mashed potatoes and reduce the baking time to 15 to 20 minutes. Serve the potatoes right in the cups.

The above amount will fill 8 cups.

Baked Potatoes

Baked potatoes are delicious, nutritious, and *easy*. The only thing you have to remember is that you must *always* prick the skin of the potato before placing it in the oven. (A 2-tined fork is best for this.) Most beginning cooks have a potato explode in the oven before they remember how important this little step is.

baking potatoes*
butter
salt and pepper

Utensils needed:
scrubbing brush

1. Heat oven to 425 degrees.
2. Scrub the potatoes well with a brush and prick the skins with a fork to allow steam to escape from the potatoes when baking.
3. If you prefer crispy skins, rub the potatoes with a little cooking oil.
4. Bake the potatoes on a rack in the middle of the oven for 40 to 60 minutes.
5. When it is cooked, gently roll the hot potato with your hand on a smooth surface to make the inside light and mealy.
6. Cut a criss-cross in the top with a sharp knife and press the sides to further open the top.
7. Drop in a spoonful of butter and salt and pepper to taste.

Hint: To speed up cooking time, insert a 2-inch nail lengthwise into the raw potato, then bake.

Variation — Foil-Baked Potatoes

Scrub the potatoes, dry them, then wrap individually in foil. Bake at 350 degrees for 1½ hours.

* These should be big and uniform in size so they will all be cooked at the same time.

Roast Potatoes

Even a number of experienced cooks have not learned the secret of making the very best roast potatoes: you have to boil them first, but only for 5 minutes, before roasting in the oven.

4 medium potatoes
¼ teaspoon salt
2 tablespoons oil
2 tablespoons butter
salt and pepper
paprika

Utensils needed:
vegetable peeler
saucepan
shallow baking dish

1. Heat the oven to 350 degrees. If you will be making the potatoes to serve with a roast, start preparing the potatoes about 1¼ hours before serving time.
2. Peel the potatoes.
3. Place in a saucepan, cover with cold water, and add salt. Bring to a boil over high heat. Boil for 5 minutes, then remove from heat and drain well.
4. Mix oil and butter in the bottom of a shallow baking dish. Mixture should cover the pan well.
5. Place the potatoes in the pan, rolling them around to coat with oil and butter. (Or you may want to arrange them around the roast, turning once to coat with beef drippings.)
6. Sprinkle with salt and pepper to taste, and paprika. The paprika is important, for that is what is going to give them their golden brown appearance.
7. Bake for 30 minutes. Turn the potatoes over, and bake for a further 30 minutes, or until tender when pierced with a fork.

Serves 4.

Scalloped Potatoes

This is an invaluable recipe. It is very easy to assemble, tastes great, and goes with just about anything.

2 medium potatoes
2 medium onions
1 can cream of mushroom
  soup (10 oz.)
½ soup can of milk

Utensils needed:
vegetable peeler
8″ baking dish
can opener

1. Turn oven to 350 degrees.
2. Peel the potatoes and slice one of them crossways to cover the bottom of the baking dish.
3. Peel the onions. Slice one thinly and place on top of potato layer.
4. Slice second potato and place on top of onion layer.
5. Slice remaining onion thinly and layer over potato.
6. Stir soup and milk together and pour over potatoes and onions.
7. Bake, *covered,* for 1 hour or until potatoes are soft when pierced with a fork.

Serves 3 to 4.

Note: If this is going to be served to guests, dress it up by sprinkling some chopped green pepper and chopped pimiento over the potatoes before pouring the soup over.

Quick Potatoes Romanoff

The Potatoes Romanoff of yesteryear demanded the tedious job of grating cold boiled potatoes, but through the magic of modern technology we are now blessed with frozen, ready-made hash browns. Try to find hash browns that most resemble grated potatoes.

1 package frozen hash
  browns (1 lb.)
4 green onions
1 tablespoon butter
¼ teaspoon seasoning salt
1 can cream of chicken soup
  (10 oz.)
1 cup sour cream
1 cup grated Cheddar cheese
2 tablespoons grated
  Parmesan cheese
paprika

Utensils needed:
grater
can opener
medium bowl
9″ casserole

1. Allow potatoes to thaw slightly in the bag.
2. Turn oven to 350 degrees. Butter the casserole.
3. Chop the onions and melt the butter.
4. Combine onion, butter, salt, soup, and sour cream in a bowl.
5. Add grated Cheddar cheese and partly thawed potatoes.
6. Mix together well, then transfer to the buttered casserole.
7. Sprinkle with Parmesan cheese and a dash of paprika, if desired.
8. Bake uncovered for 35 minutes. Remove potatoes from oven and let them sit for 10 to 15 minutes, covered with foil, before serving.

Serves 4 to 6.

Variation

These are excellent prepared a day ahead and refrigerated until cooking time. After sprinkling on the Parmesan and paprika, cover the casserole and place in the refrigerator. About 55 minutes before serving time, heat the oven to 350 degrees. When indicator light shows oven has reached required temperature, uncover casserole and place in the oven to bake for 45 minutes. Serve immediately.

Fluffy Rice

If you are a newcomer to cooking rice, the safest method is oven-baking. It is foolproof.

1 cup long-grain rice,
  uncooked
2 cups boiling water
2 tablespoons butter
½ teaspoon salt

Utensils needed:
2-quart casserole

1. Heat oven to 350 degrees.
2. Place all ingredients in a buttered 2-quart casserole.
3. Cover with lid or foil and bake for 45 minutes.
4. Fluff with a fork just before serving.

Serves 4.

Variation

For more flavorful rice, dissolve 2 teaspoons instant chicken bouillon powder in the boiling water before adding.

Spanish Rice in Foil

If you hate washing dishes, this one's for you.

1¼ cups rice, uncooked
1¼ cups diced green pepper
1¼ cups chopped green
  onion
1¼ cups diced celery
salt and pepper
1 can tomatoes (28 oz.)

Utensils needed:
can opener
aluminum foil
measuring cup
cookie sheet

1. Turn oven to 400 degrees.
2. Cut 5 pieces of foil, each approximately 1 foot square when folded in half.
3. Place ¼ cup of rice and vegetables on each double sheet of foil.
4. Sprinkle with salt and pepper to your taste.
5. Drain the tomatoes, reserving the juice in a measuring cup. Add 2 whole tomatoes to each "package" of rice.
6. Bring two opposite sides of the foil up and seal with a double fold. Seal one end as well, with a double fold.
7. Pour ¼ cup reserved tomato juice into the open end of each foil envelope. Fold end over to seal.
8. Put package on a cookie sheet and bake for 30 minutes at 400 degrees.

Serves 5.

Variations

To make this a complete meal, add ¼ cup lean ground beef and ¼ cup mushrooms to each packet before adding the tomatoes.

This recipe is great done on the barbecue, but to ensure that the rice doesn't burn, slip a section of damp paper towel between the layers of foil.

Chinese Snow Pea Pods

To prepare pea pods for cooking, cut the tips and tails off using scissors. If peas are a little mature, remove the stringy spine. If they are young and tender, there will be no stringy spine.

1 tablespoon oil
½ pound fresh snow pea
   pods
½ teaspoon sugar
garlic salt
pepper
ginger

Utensils needed:
wok or large fry pan

1. Heat the oil over high heat in a wok or large fry pan.
2. Add the pea pods, sugar, a light sprinkling of garlic salt and pepper, and a pinch (as much as you can hold between your thumb and forefinger) of ginger.
3. Cover and cook for only a minute or two. You want the pea pods to be tender, but still crisp.

Serves 4 to 5.

Variation

If you want to dress these up for guests, add 1 cup sliced fresh mushrooms and a small can of water chestnuts, drained and thinly sliced. Place in pan with pea pods and cook all together.

If you are using frozen snow peas, rinse in cold water to thaw, then pat dry.

Broiled Tomatoes

A broiled tomato half is so useful when designing a meal, as much for color as for taste and convenience. Choose firm, ripe tomatoes with a good bright red color.

tomatoes
celery salt
black pepper
sugar

Utensils needed:
pie plate or shallow
   baking dish

1. Turn broiler on to preheat.
2. Wash the tomatoes and cut in half.
3. Sprinkle the cut side with celery salt (if you have no celery salt, use regular salt), black pepper (freshly ground, if possible), and a pinch of sugar.
4. Place under broiler for about 8 to 10 minutes, leaving oven door open. Check occasionally to make sure they are not burning.

Serve half a tomato per person.

Variation

These may be dressed up by sprinkling with grated cheese (Parmesan, Cheddar, or Swiss) or with buttered bread crumbs before placing under broiler.

Baked Tomato Halves

These are so colorful they'll perk up any meal that seems to lack pizzazz.

2 firm large tomatoes
celery salt
½ cup Miracle Whip
1 tablespoon crumbled bacon
  or bacon chips
1 tablespoon chopped green
  onion

Utensils needed:
pie plate or shallow baking
  dish

1. Turn oven to 325 degrees. Butter the pie plate.
2. Cut the tomatoes in half.
3. Sprinkle the cut side with celery salt.
4. Place tomato halves in the greased pie plate, cut side up.
5. Divide the salad dressing among the tomato halves, covering the top.
6. Sprinkle with the onion and crumbled bacon.
7. Bake in the oven for 20 minutes. Do not overcook or tomatoes will lose their shape and become mushy.

Serves 4.

Mashed Turnip

We have given the recipe for a whole turnip because, like the cabbage, it is not possible to buy one-half or part of a turnip. Don't worry, though, this dish reheats very well. Any leftover portion may be reheated in a day or two or frozen.

1 small turnip
  (about 2 lb.)
½ teaspoon salt
2 tablespoons brown sugar
1 tablespoon butter
pinch of nutmeg

Utensils needed:
medium saucepan
potato masher or food
  processor

1. Peel and dice the turnip.
2. Place in a saucepan and cover with cold water.
3. Add salt and sugar and stir in until sugar is melted.
4. Turn heat to high. When water comes to a boil, cover the pot with a lid, turn heat to medium, and cook turnip until it is tender. This will take about 25 minutes. Turnip is cooked when a fork enters the turnip pieces easily.
5. Drain turnip and mash well. (This may be done in a food processor if you have one.) When turnip is well mashed, stir in butter and nutmeg.
6. Return to heat briefly to make sure it is well heated.

Serves 4 to 6.

Variation

The addition of applesauce has converted many a turnip-hater. When you have mashed the cooked turnip, add 1 cup of applesauce along with the butter and nutmeg. If you plan to add applesauce, omit the brown sugar in the cooking process.

Baked Zucchini

This popular vegetable is showing up everywhere — in cookies, cakes (see Carrot Zucchini Cake on page 185), soups, meat loaves and hamburger patties, to name a few. It is low in calories and high in vitamins A and C. We will give you a very simple and excellent way of preparing it so you can serve it often. Choose firm, rather small ones — 6 to 7 inches in length and about 2 inches in width is a perfect size and will serve two nicely.

2 zucchini
1½ tablespoons melted
   butter
1½ tablespoons grated
   Parmesan cheese
salt and pepper

Utensils needed:
shallow baking dish

1. Turn oven to 350 degrees or preheat the broiler if you are pressed for time and would prefer to broil it.
2. Wash the zucchini.
3. Leave skin on but slice both ends off and discard.
4. Cut zucchini in half lengthwise and score the cut side with a knife. (This means take a sharp knife and make slashes on the diagonal about quarter-way into the flesh; turn and do the same in the opposite direction so you have created "diamonds" about ½ inch wide.)
5. Brush the cut surface with melted butter, sprinkle with salt (seasoning salt is nice), pepper, and Parmesan cheese.
6. Place in a 350-degree oven for 30 minutes.
7. If you prefer to broil it, place under a preheated broiler for 10 minutes. (Remember, oven door open.)

Serves 3 to 4.

Note: These timings are for tender-crisp zucchini, which is the best way to serve it.

Cookies & Squares

Chocolate Peanut Clusters
Dad's Cookies
Almond Squares
Special K Bars
Lemon Squares
Brownies
Scottish Shortbread Fingers
Peanut Butter Cookies

Helpful Hint

Store all broken cookies and cookie crumbs in a sealed
container. Make a pie crust out of them by blending 1½ cups
crushed crumbs with ⅓ cup melted butter. Press into the bottom
of a pie plate, chill, then fill with pie filling.

Chocolate Peanut Clusters

No bake — and delicious. Wise to double this recipe; they disappear quickly.

1 small package semi-sweet chocolate chips (6 oz.)
1 small package butterscotch chips (6 oz.)
2 cups peanuts, any kind
2 cups chow mein noodles*

Utensils needed:
double boiler
cookie sheet

1. Boil water in the bottom of the double boiler. (A double boiler is simply a smaller saucepan set in a larger one. In the larger one — the bottom — you have boiling water, and in the smaller one — the top — place the ingredients you want to cook. So if you don't have a proper double boiler, a smaller saucepan set in a larger one will suffice.)
2. In the top of the double boiler, melt chocolate and butterscotch chips. Remove from heat when melting is complete.
3. Add peanuts and noodles. Mix thoroughly.
4. Spread wax paper over a cookie sheet, waxed side up.
5. Drop mixture by teaspoonfuls onto wax paper.
6. Allow to set either on the counter or in the refrigerator.
7. Store in a cool place.

  * Generally found in Chinese food section of the supermarket.

Dad's Cookies

Just like Mom used to make and Dad used to love.

1 cup margarine
1 cup white sugar
½ cup brown sugar
1 egg
¾ cup flaked coconut
1 teaspoon vanilla
1½ cups all-purpose flour
1 teaspoon baking soda
1 teaspoon baking powder

Utensils needed:
large bowl
electric mixer
cookie sheet
spatula

1. Turn oven to 350 degrees.
2. With the mixer, beat margarine until creamy. (This takes 2 to 3 minutes.)
3. Add sugars, then egg, and beat well.
4. Add remainder of ingredients, mixing well.
5. Drop mixture by teaspoonfuls onto a cookie sheet. Set them quite far apart (about 2″), as the cookies will spread a bit while baking.
6. Bake for 12 to 15 minutes.
7. Remove from the cookie sheet with a spatula while cookies are still warm.

Makes 3 dozen.

Variation

To make Dad's Oatmeal Cookies, add 1¼ cups oatmeal.

Almond Squares

Base

1½ cups all-purpose flour
3 tablespoons icing sugar
½ cup butter

Utensils needed:
electric mixer or food
  processor
9″ x 13″ baking pan
small saucepan

1. Heat oven to 350 degrees.
2. Place all of the above ingredients in the small bowl of an electric mixer (or in a food processor). Turn mixer to medium speed until ingredients are mixed to a crumbly stage, like cornmeal.
3. Empty crumbled mixture into the baking pan and, using your hands, press mixture firmly and evenly into the bottom of the pan.
4. Place in heated oven and bake for 12 minutes.
5. Remove from oven, but leave oven on.

Middle

1 package sliced almonds (3½ oz.)

1. Sprinkle almonds evenly over cooked base.

Top

½ cup cereal cream
  (half and half)
2 tablespoons butter
1⅔ cups brown sugar
1½ teaspoons vanilla

1. Place all of the ingredients for topping in a small saucepan; stir to dissolve sugar.
2. Place saucepan on burner and turn to medium-high. When mixture starts to boil, turn to medium-low and boil for 5 minutes.
3. Remove from heat and pour over almonds.
4. Return to the 350-degree oven and bake for 10 minutes.
5. When cool, cut in squares.

Makes 24 squares.

Special K Bars

Just the thing to pack along for hiking or camping — nutritious and energy-giving. For a healthful variation, try substituting granola for the Special K.

¼ cup sugar
½ cup corn syrup
¾ cup peanut butter
½ teaspoon vanilla
3 cups Special K cereal
1 package semi-sweet
   chocolate chips (6 oz.)

Utensils needed:
small saucepan
large bowl
9″ square baking pan

1. Place sugar, corn syrup, and peanut butter in a small saucepan and heat gently, stirring occasionally until mixture is well blended.
2. Remove from heat and stir in vanilla.
3. Place cereal in a large mixing bowl and pour peanut butter mixture over.
4. Stir until cereal is coated with peanut butter mixture.
5. Butter the baking pan, then pack mixture evenly in pan with your fingers. (If you butter your fingers, you will find it easier to pack down.)
6. When this has cooled, melt chocolate chips over low heat, then spread on top of cereal base. Let cool before cutting in squares. Keep in a cool place.

Makes 16 squares.

Lemon Squares

Lemony!

Base

1 cup all-purpose flour
¼ cup icing sugar
½ cup butter

Utensils needed:
small bowl
electric mixer
8″ square baking pan

1. Turn oven to 350 degrees.
2. Blend flour, icing sugar, and butter in a small bowl until well mixed. You may do this with an electric mixer or just use your fingers to rub the butter into the flour and sugar mixture.
3. Pat evenly into the bottom of a baking pan.
4. Bake in a 350 degree oven for 20 minutes.
5. Remove from oven to cool, but leave oven on.

Top

1 cup sugar
pinch of salt
½ teaspoon baking powder
2 eggs
2½ tablespoons lemon juice
1 teaspoon grated lemon rind

1. Place all of these ingredients in a bowl and beat until well blended.
2. Pour over cooled crust. Return to oven for 20 to 25 minutes until top is set. When it is cooked, the top should not jiggle.
3. Remove from oven and cool.
4. When cool, sprinkle the top with sifted icing sugar and cut into squares.

Makes 16 squares.

Brownies

Everybody has to know how to make brownies sooner or later.

¾ cup all-purpose flour
5 tablespoons cocoa
1 cup sugar
½ teaspoon salt
½ cup soft butter or
  margarine
2 eggs
¼ cup chopped walnuts
1 teaspoon vanilla

Utensils needed:
sifter
electric mixer
8″ square baking pan

1. Turn oven to 350 degrees. Grease and flour an 8-inch square baking pan.
2. Sift flour, cocoa, sugar, and salt together into large bowl of mixer.
3. Add all of the remaining ingredients and beat with mixer at medium speed for 3 minutes.
4. Spread mixture in the baking pan.
5. Bake in preheated oven for 30 minutes.
6. Remove pan from oven to cool, then top with chocolate frosting.

Chocolate Frosting

¾ cup icing sugar
¼ cup cocoa
2 tablespoons soft butter
1 teaspoon vanilla
1 tablespoon cereal cream
  (half and half)

1. Combine all ingredients in a small bowl and beat until good spreading consistency.

Topping Variations

As soon as brownies come out of the oven, arrange 8 to 10 chocolate mint patties on top and pop back in oven for 3 minutes, or until patties are soft enough to spread over entire top.

Melt a 6-oz. package of semi-sweet chocolate chips and 1/2 cup chunky peanut butter together over medium heat, until smooth and spreadable. Spread on cooled brownies.

Scottish Shortbread Fingers

Although shortbread is traditionally a Christmas treat, these are so easy to make, you find yourself making them in July. You *must* use real butter.

¾ pound butter
¾ cup icing sugar
3 cups all-purpose flour

Utensils needed:
large bowl
electric mixer
cookie sheet

1. Leave butter in a large bowl out of refrigerator overnight to soften (critical to this recipe).
2. Heat oven to 325 degrees.
3. Using an electric mixer, beat softened butter until smooth and creamy, for about 2 minutes.
4. Gradually add icing sugar, beating continuously.
5. Add flour gradually as well.
6. With clean hands, remove the soft dough from the bowl and transfer to a cookie sheet or jelly roll pan.
7. Pat and press with your fingers until dough covers pan.
8. Prick all over the surface with a fork and press the tip of a teaspoon into dough around the edges of the pan (fluting).
9. Bake at 325 degrees for 20 minutes.
10. Remove from oven and, while still hot, sprinkle lightly with granulated sugar and cut into finger-size lengths. (Cut lengthwise into 4 pieces, then widthwise into 4 pieces, then cut each section into 3 or 4 more pieces.)

Yields 4 dozen.

Peanut Butter Cookies

(No flour!)

A glass of cold milk, a plate of these cookies, and a good book is heaven (also nutritious!).

1 cup smooth-style peanut
  butter
1 cup brown sugar
1 egg
1 teaspoon vanilla
pinch of salt
⅓ cup crushed shredded
  wheat (1 large biscuit)

Utensils needed:
medium bowl
electric mixer or wooden
  spoon
cookie sheet
spatula
cake cooler

1. Turn oven to 325 degrees.
2. Combine all ingredients in a medium-size bowl until well mixed. (Crumble the shredded wheat with your hands before adding.) Mixture will be a little drier than most cookie doughs but don't be tempted to add any liquid.
3. Using your hands, roll dough into small balls about 1 inch in diameter and place 2½ inches apart on an ungreased cookie sheet.
4. Flatten balls with a fork. Each should now measure 2 inches in diameter. Dip the fork in a glass of cold water first to keep from sticking.
5. Bake for 13 to 15 minutes or until slightly firm to the touch. (The edges will start to color very, very slightly.)
6. Remove cookie sheet from oven. Let sit for 1 or 2 minutes to "set" before removing cookies.
7. With a spatula, transfer cookies to a wire rack (cake cooler) to finish cooling.

Makes 2⅓ dozen.

Note: If you have no shredded wheat, it may be omitted. You will still end up with a quick, easy, "toothsome" cookie.

Cakes

Carrot Zucchini Cake
Beet Cake
Large Chocolate Cake
Small Chocolate Cake
No-Bake Fruitcake
Coconut Cake
Lemon Yogurt Cake

Carrot Zucchini Cake

Carrot cake's popularity has kept increasing, as has the variety of recipes. The following recipe must surely be the very latest and most nutritious, with such additions as zucchini *and* coconut *and* whole wheat flour. If you have no whole wheat flour, use all-purpose flour.

2 eggs
1 cup sugar
⅔ cup oil
¾ cup all-purpose flour
½ cup whole wheat flour
1 teaspoon baking powder
1 teaspoon baking soda
1 teaspoon cinnamon
¾ teaspoon salt
1 cup grated carrot
1 cup grated zucchini, peeled
   first
½ cup shredded coconut

Utensils needed:
grater or food processor
9″ square baking pan
large bowl
medium bowl
electric mixer

1. Turn oven to 350 degrees.
2. Grease and flour a 9″ square baking pan, or spray with a vegetable cooking spray.
3. Beat eggs with sugar in a large bowl until frothy.
4. Gradually beat in oil.
5. Combine dry ingredients, add to first mixture in the large bowl, and beat together until well mixed. Batter will be a little on the thick side.
6. Add carrot, zucchini, and coconut. Beat until well blended.
7. Pour into prepared pan.
8. Bake in the preheated oven at 350 degrees for 35 to 40 minutes, or until top springs back when lightly touched.
9. Leave in pan. Frost when cool with Cream Cheese Frosting. (See next page.)

Beet Cake

For a totally different cake, try substituting 2 cups of grated raw beets for the combined carrots and zucchini.

Cream Cheese Frosting

1 small package cream cheese,
   at room temperature
   (4 oz.)
¼ cup butter
2 cups icing sugar
1 teaspoon vanilla
1 teaspoon grated orange rind

1. Beat cream cheese and butter together until creamy.
2. Beat in icing sugar, vanilla, and orange rind until creamy. Spread on cake.

Large Chocolate Cake

If you like your chocolate cake moist, heavy, and "chocolatey," we're sure this will be a longstanding favorite.

1 package Jello Chocolate
  Pudding — not instant
  (6 oz.)
2½ cups milk
1 package devil's food
  cake mix (18 oz.)
1 cup semi-sweet chocolate
  chips

Utensils needed:
large saucepan
9" x 13" cake pan
spatula

1. Heat oven to 375 degrees.
2. Using a large saucepan, make pudding according to package directions but use 2½ cups milk instead of the quantity given on the package.
3. When pudding is cooked, remove pot from heat and add cake mix. Stir until blended.
4. Grease the cake pan.
5. Transfer batter to the cake pan, distributing the batter evenly and smoothing the top.
6. Sprinkle chocolate chips over top.
7. Bake for 25 minutes, or until the top of the cake springs back when touched with a finger. (Oven *must* have reached 375 degrees before you put the cake in; watch indicator light.)
8. Immediately after removing the cake from the oven, smooth the melted chocolate chips over with a knife (to resemble icing), though you may prefer to leave them as is for a bumpy effect. Tastes good both ways.

Small Chocolate Cake

An excellent cake with minimal effort — no creaming procedure and no greasing and flouring of the pan.

1½ cups all-purpose flour
1 cup sugar
⅓ cup cocoa
¾ teaspoon salt
1 teaspoon baking soda
1 egg
½ cup sour milk*
½ cup oil
1 teaspoon vanilla
½ cup boiling water

Utensils needed:
sifter
electric mixer
large bowl
8″ square baking pan

1. Turn oven to 325 degrees.
2. Sift all dry ingredients into a large bowl.
3. Add remaining ingredients and blend together with an electric mixer.
4. Pour into an *ungreased* 8″ square pan.
5. Bake at 325 degrees for 15 minutes. Increase temperature to 350 degrees and bake for an additional 15 minutes.
6. Remove from oven and cool in pan. Frost.

Frosting

You may frost with any frosting of your choice, but here is a very quick and easy one which makes just the right amount.

1 square unsweetened
  chocolate (1 oz.)
¼ cup butter
⅛ cup milk
1 cup icing sugar

Utensils needed:
medium saucepan
beater

1. Melt chocolate and butter in a saucepan over very low heat.
2. Add milk. Turn heat off and stir; mixture will get thick.
3. Beat in icing sugar.
4. If icing is a little too stiff to spread easily, add a bit of lemon juice or cream. (Lemon cuts down the sweet taste, so don't use too much.)

* Add 1 tablespoon of vinegar to ordinary milk and it will sour.

No-Bake Fruitcake

One of the biggest problems one is faced with when making a fruitcake is timing. Ovens vary a bit in temperature and it is difficult to give an exact baking time. If you overcook the fruitcake it is dry and crumbly, and undercooking produces a "doughy" mess. After many weeks of experimenting, we *finally* solved the problem — don't bake it!

1 pound marshmallows
1 cup sherry
1 pound raisins
1 pound chopped candied
   fruitcake mix
3 cups chopped pecans
1 cup shredded coconut
1 box graham cracker
   crumbs (14 oz.)

Utensils needed:
double boiler
large bowl
2 9" x 5" loaf pans

1. Line 2 loaf pans with foil and set aside.
2. Place marshmallows in the top of a double boiler. (See page 175 for a description of a double boiler.) Set this over simmering water in the bottom part of double boiler and, stirring occasionally, leave marshmallows over heat until melted. Stir in sherry.
3. Place all remaining ingredients in a large bowl. When the melted marshmallows and sherry are thoroughly combined, pour onto the dry ingredients and mix well. You may want to use your hand for this, as batter will be slightly heavy and sticky.
4. Divide mixture evenly between the loaf pans. Pack down well and cover with foil. Store in a cool place for about 1 week before slicing and serving.

Note: A microwave may be used for melting the marshmallows.

Coconut Cake

2 eggs
1 cup brown sugar
⅛ teaspoon baking soda
¼ cup plus 1 tablespoon
  all-purpose flour
1 teaspoon vanilla
1⅓ cups shredded coconut
2 tablespoons butter

Utensils needed:
8″ square baking pan
medium bowl

1. Turn oven to 325 degrees.
2. Break eggs into a bowl and beat with a fork until lemon-colored throughout. This will take only about 20 to 25 vigorous strokes with the fork.
3. Add the brown sugar, baking soda, flour, and vanilla; mix well with the fork — about 40 additional strokes. Stir in the coconut.
4. Place butter in the baking pan. When the red oven light has gone out, indicating that oven is at the right temperature, place the pan in the oven until butter has melted.
5. Remove pan from oven and tilt back and forth to distribute melted butter evenly.
6. Empty contents from bowl onto melted butter. Press gently to spread evenly but *do not stir.*
7. Bake for 25 minutes.

Lemon Yogurt Cake

1 package lemon cake mix
1 package Jello Lemon
  Instant Pudding (3¾ oz.)
4 eggs
1 cup unflavored yogurt
¼ cup lemon juice
¼ cup water

Utensils needed:
electric mixer
angel food cake pan*
small saucepan (for glaze)

1. Turn oven to 350 degrees.
2. Place all ingredients into large bowl of mixer and beat thoroughly for 5 minutes with mixer at medium speed.
3. Grease and flour the cake pan.
4. Empty batter into cake pan and bake in preheated oven for 55 minutes.
5. Remove from oven and cool before removing from pan. Frost or glaze with either of the following.

Lemon Butter Cream Icing

3 tablespoons butter
1 teaspoon grated
    lemon rind
¼ teaspoon salt
2½ cups icing sugar
4 tablespoons cereal cream
    (half and half)
1 teaspoon vanilla

1. Blend the butter, lemon rind, and salt.
2. Add the icing sugar gradually, ½ cup at a time, beating between each addition.
3. Add the cream and vanilla. With electric mixer at high speed, beat until the icing is creamy.
4. Spread on cooled cake.

Glaze

Easier than making an icing and adds a finishing touch to the cake.

½ cup sugar
2 tablespoons lemon juice
½ cup orange juice

1. Combine ingredients in a small saucepan.
2. Place over medium heat and stir until sugar is dissolved.
3. Pour while still warm over cooled cake.

* If you have no angel food cake pan, use a 9″ x 13″ cake pan and bake in a 350-degree oven for 35 to 45 minutes or until top springs back when lightly touched with fingers. It won't be as showy as the higher round cake, but it will taste exactly the same.

Desserts

Baked Apples
Flaky Apple Dumplings
Bachelor's Apple Pie
Apple Crisp
Peach Crumb Pie
Chocolate-Peanut Butter Pie
Tipsy Torte
Chocolate-Dipped Strawberries
Lemon Chiffon Pie
No-Crust Lemon Pie
Pecan Pie
Blueberry Cheesecake
Butterfinger Angel Food Dessert
Strawberry Shortcake
Ice Cream Pie

Helpful Hints

1. Peeled, cored, and sliced apples (like potatoes) will not discolor if immediately placed in cold salted water.

2. Spoon a little undiluted frozen orange juice over cut-up fresh fruit for a deliciously refreshing fruit salad.

3. For a "hurry up" chocolate sauce, melt some Hershey milk chocolate with almonds over hot water, then stir in a tablespoon of rum. Serve warm over vanilla ice cream.

Baked Apples

This is one of the few desserts you would bother making just for yourself, and then you would make two, one to serve hot with your dinner and the other to have cold with the following night's dinner. These are strictly family fare. If you want to dress baked apples up for guests, follow the recipe for Flaky Apple Dumplings.

apples
brown sugar
butter
cinnamon
whipping cream

Utensils needed:
apple corer
shallow baking dish

1. Turn oven to 375 degrees.
2. Wash and core the apples and place in a baking dish.
3. Cut skins at the top of the apple in an *X* to prevent skins from bursting.
4. Fill cavities with brown sugar. Top with a dab of butter and a sprinkle of cinnamon.
5. Fill baking dish with water to a depth of ¼ inch.
6. Bake for 45 to 50 minutes or until apples are tender.
7. Pour cream (unwhipped) over the apples just before serving.

Serves: 1 apple per person.

Flaky Apple Dumplings

Absolutely delicious, but quite filling. Would suggest it follow a rather light meal (or fifty push-ups!).

1 package frozen puff pastry
   dough, thawed (14½ oz.)
4 large apples
½ cup raisins
2 tablespoons chopped nuts
1½ cups brown sugar
1 cup water
sweetened whipped cream —
   optional

Utensils needed:
apple corer
rolling pin
small saucepan
shallow baking dish

1. Make sure the pastry dough is thawed. Heat oven to 400 degrees.
2. On a clean kitchen counter top, roll dough into a 16-inch square.
3. Cut into 4 squares.
4. Peel and core the apples, placing 1 on each square.
5. Mix raisins and nuts and fill apples.
6. For each square, moisten the corners with a fingertip dipped in water, then bring 2 opposite corners up over the apple and press together. Repeat with the other 2 corners so that the apple is sealed in an envelope of dough.
7. Place the apples in an ungreased baking dish.
8. Combine sugar and water in a saucepan over medium-high heat, bring to boiling, and pour around the dumplings in the dish.

9. Bake at 400 degrees for 40 minutes.
10. Spoon the syrup over the dumplings a few times during baking period.
11. Best served warm but also good cold the next day.

Serves 4.

Bachelor's Apple Pie

This could have been named "One-Dish Apple Pie," for that is all you need.

1 cup Bisquick baking mix
4 tablespoons soft butter
3 tablespoons boiling water
5 medium apples
½ cup brown sugar
1 teaspoon cinnamon
½ cup sour cream
2 tablespoons butter

Utensils needed:
apple corer
9″ pie plate

1. Heat oven to 350 degrees.
2. Mix the Bisquick, soft butter, and water in the pie plate (a fork works well), then press it evenly on the bottom and around the sides of the pie plate.
3. Cut apples into 4 sections; remove peel, then core (a melon baller is a marvelous tool for this). Slice each quarter-section into thin slices.
4. Place apple slices on top of Bisquick crust you have made.
5. Combine the sugar, cinnamon, and sour cream and distribute as evenly as you can over the top of the apples.
6. Dot with butter cut into little pieces.
7. Bake for 30 minutes.
8. Serve while still warm, with a scoop of vanilla ice cream.
9. Leftovers are great served cold the next day, but we bet you won't have any.

Apple Crisp

A great way to use up those apples that are "going."

1 cup brown sugar
¾ cup all-purpose flour
1 teaspoon cinnamon
½ cup butter or margarine
5 apples

Utensils needed:
small bowl
pastry cutter*
8″ square baking pan

1. Heat oven to 375 degrees. Butter the baking pan.
2. Mix together brown sugar, flour, and cinnamon in a small bowl.
3. Cut in butter with the pastry cutter until the mixture is the consistency of coarse bread crumbs.
4. Peel and slice the apples.
5. Combine one-quarter of the crumb mixture with the sliced apples.
6. Place in the buttered baking pan. Sprinkle the top with remaining crumb mixture.
7. Bake for 45 minutes.
8. Serve warm with cream, whipped cream, or ice cream.

Serves 6.

Variation

Rushed? Substitute a can of apple pie filling for the apples, and either cut out or cut down the amount of sugar, depending on the sweetness of your tooth.

* If you don't have a pastry cutter, use 2 knives or a potato masher with large holes.

Peach Crumb Pie

Even though we consider ourselves to be experienced cooks who make not a bad pastry, we've always used the convenient ready-made pie shells for this particular recipe; that way this pie really comes under the heading of the yummiest jiffy dessert you'll ever make.

9" ready-made, frozen, deep-dish pie shell
½ cup all-purpose flour
¼ cup white sugar
¼ cup brown sugar
½ teaspoon cinnamon
¼ cup butter
½ cup chopped walnuts or pecans
1 can peaches (14 oz.)

Utensils needed:
pastry cutter or 2 knives
small bowl
can opener

1. Thaw the pie shell. (Do not prick the crust.)
2. Turn oven on to 450 degrees.
3. In a small bowl, mix the flour, sugars, and cinnamon.
4. Using a pastry cutter if you have one, or simply 2 knives, cut the butter into the flour mixture until butter pieces are about the size of a pea.
5. Spread approximately half of this mixture in the bottom of the pie shell.
6. Add the chopped nuts to the rest of the mixture in the bowl.
7. Drain liquid from the peaches and slice them. (Either discard or drink the drained juice; you will not need it for this recipe.)
8. Arrange the peach slices in the pie crust.
9. Top with remaining flour mixture.
10. Bake at 450 degrees for 10 minutes, then turn oven down to 350 degrees and continue baking for 20 minutes.
11. Serve warm with a scoop of vanilla ice cream.

Serves 5 to 6.

Chocolate-Peanut Butter Pie

Definitely what we'd suggest the day before the diet begins. This dessert keeps very well in the freezer — ready to be brought out for an emergency (which could be a sweet snack attack!).

Crumb Crust:

1¼ cups graham wafer crumbs or chocolate wafer crumbs
¼ cup brown sugar (packed)
⅓ cup margarine or butter, melted

Utensils needed:
9″ pie plate
can opener (unless you use bottled syrup or sauce)

Filling:

1 quart (about 4 cups) chocolate ice cream
1 cup peanut butter (smooth)
1 cup Hershey's Chocolate Syrup
1 cup peanuts

1. Mix together the crumbs and brown sugar.
2. Add melted butter or margarine.
3. Stir well with a fork, then pat firmly into bottom and up the sides of a buttered 9″ pie plate.
4. Place pie shell in freezer to set firmly.
5. Meanwhile, take ice cream out of freezer to soften *slightly* (for easier spreading).
6. When pie shell is well chilled, spoon half of ice cream into shell and pat down firmly.
7. Return pie to freezer until ice cream is set.
8. Remove from freezer and spread with a thin layer of peanut butter (about 1/2 cup).
9. Drizzle with half the chocolate sauce.
10. Sprinkle with half the peanuts.

11. Repeat the layers.
12. Return to freezer.

To serve: Remove pie from freezer 10 minutes before cutting. Add a dollop of whipping cream to each portion, or heat additional chocolate syrup to pour over. (If waistlines will allow, by all means use both!)

Tipsy Torte

Great fun to serve. Only you will know the ease with which it was made, and your friends will have a great time guessing about the ingredients. We've served this to guests numerous times and have yet to find a guest who has guessed right!

1 pint whipping cream
½ cup milk
⅓ cup Tia Maria or Kahlùa
1 package chocolate chip
  cookies
1 square semi-sweet
  chocolate, shaved (grated)

Utensils needed:
electric mixer or hand beater
small bowl
8″ spring-form pan or
  9″ square glass baking dish

1. Whip the cream with chilled beaters until stiff. This takes about 2 minutes with an electric mixer and a bit longer with a hand beater.
2. In a small bowl, combine the liqueur and milk.
3. Butter the spring-form pan or square baking dish.
4. Dip each cookie quickly in the liqueur-and-milk mixture, but do not soak.
5. Set cookies side by side in the bottom of the pan until it is covered. Fill in empty spots with dipped broken cookies.
6. Spread a layer of whipped cream over the cookies.
7. Repeat layers until the pan is full or all the cookies are used, ending with the whipped cream.
8. Top with a sprinkling of shaved chocolate. (Grating the chocolate against a potato peeler is a quick and easy way to get shaved chocolate.)
9. Refrigerate at least 6 hours or overnight.

Serves 6 to 8.

Chocolate-Dipped Strawberries

These make a great "finger food" dessert. Don't wash the berries. It is illegal to spray berries with insecticide, so they are perfectly safe to eat. If there is any sand or surface dirt, just wipe with a clean cloth.

whole strawberries, with
   stems
1 large package semi-sweet
   chocolate chips (12 oz.)
6 tablespoons butter or
   margarine

Utensils needed:
wax paper
cookie sheet
double boiler*

1. Have clean, perfect strawberries ready on a sheet of wax paper. Have the wax paper, in turn, sitting on a cookie sheet, for you have to transport the berries to the refrigerator.
2. Melt the chocolate chips in the top of a double boiler over hot (not boiling) water.
3. Stir in the butter and keep stirring until butter is melted and well mixed with the chocolate.
4. Dip strawberries in the chocolate, swirling to coat evenly, but leave the very top of the berry, below the stem, uncovered. It looks more attractive to see a bit of the berry. Work quickly before the chocolate hardens, and start with the biggest berries because they will need deeper chocolate than the smaller ones.
5. Place berries on the wax paper after dipping and refrigerate until serving time.

Variation — Strawberries Dipped in Sour Cream and Brown Sugar

Another popular "finger" strawberry dessert is made by having a platter of strawberries served with 2 small bowls in the center of the table, one filled with sour cream and the other with brown sugar. One first dips the strawberry into the sour cream, then into the sugar.

Note: If some of the berries are without stems, insert a cocktail pick into the area where the stem would be to enable you to hold the berry for dipping.

* For a description of a double boiler, see page 175.

Lemon Chiffon Pie (the easy way!)

1 can condensed milk
1 can frozen lemonade
  concentrate, thawed
  (6 oz.)
2 tablespoons fresh lemon
  juice
½ teaspoon grated lemon
  rind, optional
1 carton Cool Whip
  (16 oz.-size — which
  is 2 cups)

Utensils needed:
can opener
9″ pie plate
grater (optional)

1. Combine above ingredients with a wire whisk and empty
   into a 9″ graham cracker crust (see recipe for Crumb Crust
   in Chocolate-Peanut Butter Pie recipe on page 200; reserve
   2 tablespoons crumbs for sprinkling on top of pie).
2. Place in freezer until serving time (for a minimum of 3 hours).

Serves 6.

No-Crust Lemon Pie

Not every dessert is a party dessert. There are some excellent "family" desserts, such as the following. Good warm or chilled, plain or with whipped cream.

4 eggs
¾ cup lemon juice
1 tablespoon grated lemon
   peel
1 cup milk
1 cup sugar
¼ cup butter, diced
½ cup Bisquick baking mix

Utensils needed:
grater
10″ pie plate
blender or food processor

1. Turn oven on to 350 degrees. Butter a 10-inch pie plate.
2. Place all ingredients into blender (the type with a wide bottom) or food processor, and blend until thoroughly mixed — at least 2 full minutes.
3. Pour into the buttered pie plate and bake for 40 to 45 minutes, or until pie is set. Test it by sticking a knife in the center; it should come out clean if pie is ready.

Serves 6.

Pecan Pie

If you don't have to worry about the pastry, pecan pie is likely one of the easiest pies to make. If you cheat and use a ready-made frozen pie shell, this filling is so good no one will notice that the pie crust is not homemade. The secret of a good pecan pie is not to beat the filling with a rotary beater, only with a fork.

9″ ready-made, frozen deep-
   dish pie shell
3 eggs
1 cup sugar
¼ teaspoon salt
1 cup dark corn syrup
¼ cup melted butter
1 cup pecans

Utensils needed:
medium bowl
fork

1. Thaw the pie shell.
2. Heat the oven to 375 degrees.
3. In a medium-size bowl, beat the eggs with a fork.
4. Add the sugar, salt, syrup, and melted butter. Beat with a fork until well mixed.
5. Add pecans.
6. Transfer to the unbaked pie shell. Bake for 45 minutes, or until a knife inserted into the filling comes out clean.
7. Serve with whipped cream or, better still, whipped cream with a dash of brandy in it.

Blueberry Cheesecake

Not as "cheese-cakey" as most cheesecakes, but creamy and rich.

Crust

2¼ cups graham wafer
  crumbs
⅓ cup sugar, white or brown
⅓ cup melted butter
dash of cinnamon

Utensils needed:
medium bowl
9″ x 13″ baking dish
electric mixer
can opener

1. Combine all ingredients for the crust in a mixing bowl.
2. Mix together well and pat into a baking dish.
3. Refrigerate while you prepare the filling.

Filling

1 envelope Dream Whip
1 package cream cheese
  (8 oz.)
1 can blueberry pie filling
  (19 oz.)

1. Prepare Dream Whip according to package directions.
2. Add cream cheese and beat with a mixer until light and fluffy.
3. Remove crumb crust from refrigerator. Spread cheese mixture on top to cover crust completely.
4. Spread blueberry pie filling on top of cheese layer.*
5. Refrigerate 2 to 3 hours before serving.

Serves 10 to 12.

Variations

Add 1 cup frozen blueberries to the pie filling before spreading it.

Add a teaspoon of grated orange rind to the crumb crust for an extra bit of zip.

Try different toppings. Cherry and pineapple pie filling are excellent substitutes for the blueberry.

Note: Do not substitute whipped cream for the Dream Whip; it won't have enough body and it becomes watery after a while.

* The pie filling will be easier to apply if the cheesecake is placed in the freezer long enough to firm up — 30 minutes to an hour.

Butterfinger Angel Food Dessert

Such a cinch to whip up but absolutely scrumptious, so be ready for compliments. Best made the night before.

1 ready-made angel food cake (10″)	Utensils needed: cake plate
4 Butterfinger bars	electric mixer or hand beater
2 small cartons whipping cream (½ pt. each)	small bowl

1. Slice the cake in half so you have a top and bottom layer. Set the bottom layer on a cake plate.
2. Break up the Butterfinger bars into small pieces, but not crumbs.
3. Whip the cream with chilled beaters until stiff (about 2 minutes with a mixer and a bit longer by hand).
4. Add Butterfinger pieces to whipped cream and stir.
5. Spread the whipped cream mixture on the top of the bottom layer of the cake, set the remaining layer on top, then ice the top and sides of the cake, using all the cream mixture.
6. Chill in the refrigerator for at least 4 hours.
7. An extra, crumbled Butterfinger bar may be sprinkled on top of the cake as an attractive garnish.

Strawberry Shortcake

High on the list of favorite desserts. Everyone has their own preferred way to serve it. Here is one simple way.

2⅓ cups Bisquick baking mix
3 tablespoons sugar
3 tablespoons melted
  margarine or butter
½ cup milk
2 small cartons fresh
  strawberries
1 tablespoon sugar
1 carton whipping cream
  (1/2 pt.)
1 teaspoon sugar
1 teaspoon vanilla

Utensils needed:
medium bowl
8″ round cake pan
small deep bowl
electric mixer or hand beater

1. Heat oven to 425 degrees.
2. Combine baking mix, 3 tablespoons sugar, margarine, and milk in a bowl. Mix until a soft dough forms.
3. Spread evenly in an ungreased round baking pan.
4. Bake 15 to 20 minutes or until golden brown.
5. Wash, hull, and slice the strawberries. Sprinkle with 1 tablespoon sugar.
6. When cake is baked, remove from oven. Cool in the pan on a rack for 10 minutes, then cut into 6 wedges.
7. Pour whipping cream into a chilled bowl. Whip until cream starts to thicken. Add 1 teaspoon sugar and the vanilla and continue beating until cream starts to form stiff peaks. (Having the beaters chilled hastens the procedure.)
8. To serve, split each wedge in half. Set the bottom half on a dessert plate and spoon some of the strawberries over it, then place the other half on top and spoon on more strawberries. Mound whipped cream on the very top.

Serves 6.

Variations

Most supermarkets carry ready-made sponge cakes, angel food cakes, or individual sponge cakes, all of which may be used as your cake base. If you are a whipped cream addict, you may like to whip an additional carton of whipping cream and put whipped cream between the layers as well.

Ice Cream Pie

Make this as far ahead as you like. A big hit with young and old alike.

½ **pound peanut brittle**
1 **quart vanilla ice cream**
1 **bottle butterscotch syrup**
  (**like Smucker's**)

Utensils needed:
10″ **pie plate**

1. Crush the peanut brittle.
2. Soften the ice cream enough to mix in the peanut brittle. Don't fold in all of the peanut brittle — save some to decorate the top, about 1/2 cup.
3. Press the mixture into a lightly buttered pie plate, sprinkle with "saved" peanut brittle, cover with plastic wrap, and store in the freezer until ready to use.
4. At serving time, heat the butterscotch syrup and pass separately with wedges of ice cream.

   Serves 8. For smaller servings, see variation below.

Variation

Form ice cream into balls (an ice cream scoop is helpful for this purpose) and roll in crushed peanut brittle or chopped pecans. Freeze balls on a cookie sheet; when solidly frozen, transfer to plastic bags for storing in the freezer. These are handy to have on hand, but make sure you have a bottle of syrup on the shelf.

For Entertaining
Appetizers & Hors d'Oeuvres

"No Cook" Antipasto
Cheese Wafers
Crab & Cheese Platter
Cheese Ball
Marinated Mushrooms
Stuffed Mushroom Caps
Baked Shrimp & Cheese Dip
Nachos
Poor Man's Baked Cheese Dip
Taco Dips
Dill Dip
Spinach Dip in Hollowed-Out Loaf
Grab Bag Dip
Curry Dip
English Muffin Wedges
"No Cook" Liver Paté
Fancy Liver Paté
Salmon Paté

Helpful Hints

1. Dip water chestnuts in Parmesan cheese, then wrap each in a slice of bacon. Secure with a toothpick and bake at 400 degrees until the bacon is cooked. Delicious!

2. Never wash mushrooms — they become watery. They are grown in sterile soil so they are not "dirty." Brush them with a soft cloth or paper towel. If you are a real mushroom lover it will be worth investing in a mushroom brush. If the mushrooms are slightly old and discolored, peel them.

"No Cook" Antipasto

This is the very easiest antipasto for a beginner to tackle. If you know how to chop and stir, you can make this delicious appetizer, which will keep for two months under refrigeration. With a box of crackers on the shelf and a jar of antipasto in the refrigerator, you are never stuck for a quick hors d'oeuvre.

1 small bottle ketchup
1 bottle chili sauce
  (10 oz.)
1 jar sweet mixed pickles
  (12 oz.)
1 jar stuffed green olives
  (10 oz.)
1 can black olives (10 oz.)
1 can whole mushrooms
  (10 oz.)
1 jar cocktail onions, smallest
  size (5 oz.)
2 cans tuna (6.5 oz. each)

Utensils needed:
can opener
large bowl
sterilized jars for storage

1. Empty ketchup and chili sauce into a large bowl.
2. Drain the pickles, olives, and mushrooms well. Chop into fairly small pieces and add to ketchup and chili.
3. Drain onions, cut in half, and add to the above.
4. Drain tuna well and stir in.
5. When all the ingredients are well combined, spoon into sterilized jars and store in the refrigerator.

Hint: Save the pickle juice and pour over drained canned beets. Store in refrigerator for Instant Pickled Beets!

Cheese Wafers

These versatile little "cookies" can be served with cocktails, at a wine-and-cheese party, with tomato juice, soups, or salads. They also make a welcome gift (keep them in mind for a deserving grandmother on the next gift-giving occasion).

½ cup butter or margarine
1 cup grated Cheddar cheese
¼ teaspoon chili powder
1 cup all-purpose flour

Utensils needed:
electric mixer
small bowl
cookie sheet

1. Place butter and grated cheese in small bowl of electric mixer and beat until well combined.
2. Beat in chili powder.
3. Gradually beat in flour.
4. Empty contents of bowl onto a lightly floured piece of plastic wrap and form into a long, thin roll. Flour your hands as well, and this will help. The roll should be as long as the box of plastic wrap (if you are wondering just how long to make it).
5. Place carefully in the refrigerator to chill (use both hands to support it when you are transferring from counter to fridge; you don't want it to collapse in the middle).
6. When chilled, slice thinly (about 1/4″) and bake in a preheated 350 degree oven until the wafers are just beginning to turn a golden brown around the edges; this will take 8 to 10 minutes.

Makes 3½ dozen.

Note: These freeze well.

Crab & Cheese Platter

You will have a difficult time convincing your guests that you are a complete beginner when you appear with this gorgeous appetizer. It is one of the most attractive dips you will ever see.

2 large packages cream
  cheese (8 oz. each)
2 tablespoons lemon juice
2 tablespoons Worcestershire
  sauce
2 tablespoons mayonnaise
2 tablespoons onion flakes
1 large bottle seafood
  cocktail sauce
1 can crabmeat (6.5 oz.)

Utensils needed:
can opener
blender or electric mixer
large round platter

1. Mix together the cream cheese, lemon juice, Worcestershire sauce, mayonnaise, and onion flakes in a blender, or beat with an electric mixer, until smooth and creamy.
2. Spread cheese mixture evenly over the surface of a large round platter, leaving room around the outside for a row of crackers.
3. Press the center of the cheese mixture down lightly to make a slightly raised border, about ½ to 1 inch wide, around the outer edge.
4. Spread seafood sauce over the cheese layer within this border, so you leave an outside rim of cheese layer showing.
5. Drain the crabmeat. Spread drained crabmeat over the sauce layer, again leaving a border of seafood sauce showing.
6. Serve with crackers or vegetables.

Cheese Ball

One of the tastiest cheese balls around.

½ pound sharp
  Cheddar cheese
1 small package pimiento
  cream cheese (4 oz.)
2 teaspoons grated onion
2 tablespoons chili sauce or
  tomato ketchup
¼ teaspoon dry mustard
  powder
1 teaspoon Worcestershire
  sauce
dash of Tabasco sauce

Utensils needed:
electric mixer or food
  processor, or wooden
  spoon
small deep bowl

1. Have cheeses at room temperature.
2. Blend all ingredients together well in the mixer. (A wooden spoon will do the job as well, but it will take longer.)
3. Line a small deep bowl with plastic wrap and empty the mixed ingredients into the lined bowl.
4. Refrigerate overnight.
5. When ready to use, unmold, remove plastic wrap, and sprinkle the top with chopped nuts or chopped parsley.
6. Serve with assorted crackers.

Serves 10 to 12.

Marinated Mushrooms

Couldn't be easier or more popular, but you must use *fresh* mushrooms.

½ pound fresh mushrooms
2 green onions
½ teaspoon garlic salt
¼ cup oil

Utensils needed:
small bowl

1. Wipe the mushrooms, but do not wash them. Slice the mushrooms, with stalks, into a small bowl.
2. Chop the green onions, using mostly white part but including a little of the green. You should have ¼ cup of chopped onion.
3. Stir the garlic salt into the oil and pour over the mushrooms.
4. Stir in chopped onion.
5. Let sit in the refrigerator for 2 hours, stirring occasionally.
6. At serving time, drain well and place on fingers of lightly buttered rye bread or whole-wheat bread.

   Note: You make "fingers" of bread by trimming the crusts from bread and cutting bread slices in thirds.

Stuffed Mushroom Caps

If you live in a small community, we wouldn't suggest sharing this recipe because all your friends will be serving it when they find out how simple and foolproof it is.

1 pound fresh mushrooms
⅓ cup melted butter
1 package frozen spinach soufflé, thawed
⅓ cup grated Swiss, Cheddar, or Parmesan cheese

Utensils needed:
grater
shallow baking dish
   or pie plate

1. Turn oven to 350 degrees.
2. Wipe the mushrooms. Remove stems (save them for soup, a stir-fry, etc.) and dip caps in the melted butter. Arrange caps in a shallow baking dish or pie plate.
3. Spoon some of the thawed soufflé into each mushroom cap, enough to fill the cavity fairly generously.
4. Sprinkle with grated cheese.
5. Bake for 10 minutes. Do not overcook.
6. Serve hot.

Variation

This may also be served as a vegetable dish for a dinner party, as a superb light luncheon (especially if you can present the caps in the ceramic escargot dishes) accompanied with a salad, or as a first course. Very versatile!

Baked Shrimp & Cheese Dip

1 package Velveeta cheese
  (1 lb.)
1 can broken shrimp
  (4 oz.)
1 medium onion
½ cup Miracle Whip
1 cup grated sharp Cheddar
  cheese
2 tablespoons white wine —
  optional

Utensils needed:
grater
can opener
1-quart baking dish

1. Turn oven to 325 degrees.
2. Cube the processed cheese; drain the shrimp; and grate or finely mince the onion.
3. Combine all ingredients in an oven-proof baking dish.
4. Bake in the heated oven for 30 to 35 minutes, or until cheese is well melted, stirring once halfway through baking time.
5. Serve hot with crackers or raw vegetables as dippers.

Nachos

Nachos are fun, but some recipes are quite complicated. These two are simple to make and great to serve. One is for those who like nachos with tomato sauce, the other for those of you who consider nachos not up to par unless you breathe fire after.

Nachos — Easy and Cheesy

1 jar Cheese Whiz (16 oz.)
1 can chopped green chilis
  (4 oz.)*
1 can crushed tomatoes
  (16 oz.)
1 package tortilla chips
  (8 oz.)

Utensils needed:
2 small saucepans
can opener
oven-proof platter

1. Heat the Cheese Whiz in a saucepan until hot and melted.
2. Drain the chilis. Combine drained chilis with the undrained tomatoes in a separate saucepan. Heat until bubbly.

3. Turn broiler on.
4. Spread tortilla chips on a large oven-proof platter. Top with tomato mixture, then melted cheese.
5. Leaving oven door open, place under broiler for a few minutes until cheese bubbles.

Nachos — Hot and Simple

½ pound sharp Cheddar cheese, grated
½ pound Monterey Jack cheese, grated
4 to 6 jalapeno peppers, finely chopped*
½ cup chopped onion
1 package tortilla chips (8 oz.)

1. Heat oven to 350 degrees.
2. Mix together the cheeses, peppers, and onions.
3. Spread half the chips on an oven-proof platter. Sprinkle this layer with half the cheese mixture. Spread remaining chips over the cheese layer, then top with remaining cheese.
4. Bake for 15 to 20 minutes, or broil until hot and bubbly.

Serving Suggestion: Both kinds of nachos are good served with sour cream, guacamole, or taco sauce to dip, but you'll also like them just as is. Have lots of napkins on hand.

* Found in Mexican food section of the supermarket.

Poor Man's Baked Cheese Dip

This is about half the price of the Shrimp & Cheese Dip above, but tasty enough to serve on any occasion.

1 cup grated sharp Cheddar
  cheese
1 cup Miracle Whip
1 large onion, grated
  or finely minced

Utensils needed:
grater
1-quart baking dish

1. Turn oven to 325 degrees.
2. Combine all ingredients in an oven-proof dish, 1-quart size, and bake until brown and bubbly — about 20 to 30 minutes.
3. Serve hot with crackers or raw vegetables as dippers.

Serves 8 to 10.

Taco Dip #1

A hearty dip served with corn or taco chips. Excellent as a late-night snack with drinks. Especially popular with teenagers.

½ pound ground beef
½ cup chopped onion
1 can tomato sauce (8 oz.)
1½ teaspoons chili powder
½ teaspoon salt
1 can pork and beans
  (8 oz.)
½ cup grated Cheddar
  cheese
¼ cup sliced ripe olives

Utensils needed:
grater
can opener
large fry pan
chafing dish (or any dish
  with a warming device
  under it — candle, Sterno,
  or Salton tray)

1. Brown the ground beef over medium heat in a large skillet or fry pan.
2. Drain off any excess fat, then add *1/4 cup* onion and fry gently until transparent.
3. Stir in tomato sauce, chili powder, and salt; bring to a simmer.
4. Mash the beans, add to fry pan, and simmer a bit longer — about 5 minutes.
5. Transfer to a chafing dish. Sprinkle with cheese, olives, and the remaining 1/4 cup onion.
6. Serve hot with taco chips or corn chips.

Serves 10 to 12.

Taco Dip #2

Not as hearty as Taco Dip #1 but very easy and very tasty.

1 pound Velveeta cheese,
  cubed
2 cans chili (14 oz. each)
½ cup chopped onion

Utensils needed:
can opener
medium baking dish

1. Turn oven to 350 degrees.
2. Combine all ingredients in a medium-size baking dish and bake for 1 hour, stirring at least once during this time.
3. Remove from oven; stir well.
4. Serve hot with taco chips or corn chips.

Serves 10 to 12.

Dill Dip

We both agree that when it comes to dips for raw vegetables, you will be hard-pressed to come up with one any better than the packaged Uncle Dan's California-Style Hint of Dill Dressing mixed with ½ cup Miracle Whip and ½ cup sour cream. If you are counting calories, combine Uncle Dan's dressing with 1 cup yogurt. However, if you live in an area where you cannot purchase this mix, the following recipe rates a close second.

1 cup Miracle Whip
1 cup sour cream
1½ tablespoons onion flakes
1½ teaspoons Beau Monde seasoning
1½ teaspoons dillweed
¼ teaspoon garlic powder

Utensils needed:
small mixing bowl

1. Mix all ingredients together and refrigerate until needed.
2. Serve with assorted raw vegetables: carrot sticks, cauliflower and broccoli florets, celery sticks, mushrooms.

Serves 10 to 12.

Spinach Dip in Hollowed-Out Loaf

Very impressive — and it's hearty, healthy, and in an edible bowl. Hooray! No dish to wash!

1 round loaf of sourdough or pumpernickel bread (oval would do as well)

1 package frozen spinach (10 oz.), defrosted, drained, and chopped

1 cup mayonnaise

1 cup sour cream

1 large red onion, finely chopped

1 can water chestnuts (10 oz.), drained and chopped

1 package Hickory Farms Red Onion Dip, or any dehydrated vegetable dip of your choice

Utensils needed:
serrated-edged knife
can opener
large serving platter

1. Using a serrated-edged knife (bread knife), cut a circle out of top of loaf, leaving a 1″ edge all around the circumference.
2. Hollow out loaf and cut insides (and top of loaf) into 1″ cubes (to be used for dipping purposes).
3. Mix remaining ingredients together and spoon into hollowed-out loaf.
4. Serve on a large platter surrounded by the bread cubes.
5. Have a basket of crudités (fresh vegetables cut into finger-size pieces) or extra crackers on hand. They'll love it!

Grab Bag Dip

This is sometimes referred to as "Hidden Treasures." It may be made early in the day and kept refrigerated until serving time.

Sauce

1 cup mayonnaise
1 cup sour cream
½ cup grated horseradish
½ teaspoon salt
2 teaspoons dry mustard
  powder
2 teaspoons lemon juice

Utensils needed:
large shallow bowl or
  serving dish
can opener

1. Combine all of the above ingredients in a large shallow bowl or serving dish.

Dip

1 can whole button
  mushrooms (10 oz.)
1 can water chestnuts
  (10 oz.)
1 small jar green olives
  (8 oz.)
1 small jar black olives
  (8 oz.)
1½ pounds cooked shrimp
1 small can cooked cocktail
  sausages (4 oz.)

1. Drain the mushrooms, water chestnuts, and both jars of olives. Discard juice.
2. Add to the sauce in the bowl, together with shrimp and sausages.
3. Serve in the bowl with toothpicks or cocktail forks.

Serves 10 to 12.

Variation

For a less expensive dish, cooked meatballs (page 91) may be substituted for the shrimp. And fresh cherry tomatoes may replace the mushrooms if you want to add a bit of extra color.

Curry Dip

Except for the sour cream, the ingredients are usually on hand, making this a very valuable recipe. In a pinch, the sour cream could be omitted. This is a good dip with raw vegetables, shrimp, or meatballs.

1 cup mayonnaise
½ cup sour cream
3 tablespoons ketchup
  or chili sauce
1 tablespoon curry powder
2 teaspoons Worcestershire
  sauce
1½ teaspoons grated onion
¼ teaspoon garlic powder

Utensils needed:
small mixing bowl
large platter

1. Combine all ingredients in a mixing bowl and store in refrigerator until ready to use.
2. At serving time, place a small dish of dip in the center of a platter and surround it with assorted fresh vegetables.

Serves 10 to 12.

Hint: The vegetables will stay fresh and crisp if you place them on some cracked ice.

English Muffin Wedges

It was difficult to decide in just what section to put this recipe, as it makes a great accompaniment to soups, salads, and many casserole dishes. It is also a perfect item to feature at a morning coffee party or at a brunch. Its greatest versatility, however, lies in its role as an hors d'oeuvre. Once you combine the two major ingredients (the mayonnaise and cheese), you can substitute just about anything you have in the refrigerator (within reason!) for the bacon chips, thus changing its character considerably. For instance, some excellent choices are chopped ripe olives, chopped nuts, chopped gherkins, or chopped jalapeno peppers (be careful here — unless you have asbestos lips, you'd better stick to 1 to 2 tablespoons). For a coffee party or brunch, the bacon chips are the most appropriate.

1½ cups grated Cheddar
  cheese
½ cup mayonnaise
⅓ cup bacon chips (Do not
  substitute bacon bits,
  which are smaller and tend
  to get lost.)
8 English muffins, cut in half
  (into two circles)

Utensils needed:
grater
cookie sheet

1. Combine grated cheese, mayonnaise, and bacon chips.
2. Spread over cut side of muffins and place muffin halves on a cookie sheet under a preheated broiler for 3 to 5 minutes.
3. Cut in halves or quarters and serve hot.

Note: You may mix the mayonnaise and cheese ahead of time, but do not stir in the bacon chips until just before using, as they tend to get soggy.

"No Cook" Liver Paté

Recipes abound for liver paté where you must deal with raw chicken livers but, being a beginner, you may not be ready for that just yet. The following recipe is an excellent substitute.

½ pound liverwurst
(liver sausage)
1 small package cream
cheese (4 oz.)
1 tablespoon Miracle Whip
2 teaspoons grated onion
1 teaspoon Worcestershire
sauce
¼ teaspoon curry powder
1 tablespoon sherry or
brandy

Utensils needed:
electric mixer, food
processor, or fork

1. Blend all ingredients together. You may do this with a fork, a mixer, or a food processor.
2. Place in a serving bowl. Serve with crisp crackers; toast squares; or white, rye, or pumpernickel bread.

Note: The flavor will improve if made a day ahead. Refrigerate until serving time.

Fancy Liver Paté

The "No Cook" Liver Paté may be extended and dressed up for a larger party. In addition to the ingredients in the "No Cook" Liver Paté (preceding recipe), you will need 1 can of consommé (10 oz.) and 1 envelope of unflavored gelatin.

1. Sprinkle the gelatin over 1/2 cup of the consommé to soften. (Consommé should be at room temperature, for it gels slightly if cold.)
2. Let sit for 5 minutes. Meanwhile, heat remaining consommé in a small saucepan.
3. Dissolve gelatin mixture in the heated consommé.
4. Pour about 1/4 to 1/2 cup consommé in the bottom of a lightly oiled mold or small mixing bowl, just enough to cover the bottom. Place in refrigerator until firm. This will take about 15 to 20 minutes.

5. When the remaining consommé-gelatin mixture is lukewarm, place in blender or food processor with all the ingredients for the "No Cook" Liver Paté; blend until smooth.

6. Pour over the now-firm consommé in the mold. Cover and place in refrigerator for a minimum of 4 hours (or the dish may be made a day ahead).

7. Unmold onto a serving platter (see page 74 for how to unmold); serve with assorted crackers. The gelled consommé will form a clear brown glaze over the top of the paté when unmolded.

Salmon Paté

If you would like your guests to think you used the expensive smoked salmon to make this dish, add 1 teaspoon of Liquid Smoke to the ingredients before blending; this imitation is a dead ringer for the real thing. The paté is a wonderful way to use up any leftover cooked salmon, and it freezes well.

2 cups flaked cooked salmon*
1 package cream cheese, room temperature (8 oz.)
1 tablespoon lemon juice
1 tablespoon grated onion
¼ teaspoon salt
⅛ teaspoon black pepper**

Utensils needed:
food processor or electric mixer

1. Place all ingredients in a food processor and blend well. If you have no processor, use an electric mixer.

2. Chill for several hours to blend the flavors.

3. Serve with crackers.

Serves 10 to 12.

Note: The paté is particularly attractive when sprinkled with chopped fresh parsley just before serving.

* If you have no cooked salmon, substitute 1 large can (16 oz.) of salmon, drained.

** This is another of those recipes where using *freshly ground* black pepper makes all the difference to the taste. So do grind your own peppercorns for this, if possible.

Utensils Needed

If you have the following utensils, you can make anything and everything in this book.

Essential

Baking pans and dishes — 8" x 8" x 2"; 9" x 9" x 2"; 13" x 9" x 2"

Metal pans are called "pans." Corning Ware, Pyrex, etc. are called "dishes" or "casseroles." All of the baked goods — cakes, squares, etc. — have been tested in metal pans. We highly recommend Teflon-coated pans and have found that, after the first few uses, it is best to spray before each use with one of the vegetable oil sprays such as Mazola No-Stick or Pam. For pans requiring greasing and flouring, Baker's Joy is excellent.

Bowls for mixing — large; medium; small

Broiler pan — This comes with a rack and is usually found in every oven other than microwave or convection.

Cake cooler — You may use the rack from your broiler pan.

Can opener

Casserole dishes — 1-quart; 2-quart

Casserole dishes come in all shapes and sizes — round, square, oblong, oval — usually with a lid.

Cookie sheet

Colander — This is sometimes called a strainer.

Egg beater

Fork — Two-tined, long-handled fork for safe handling of hot foods.

Fry pan or skillet — It is best to get two sizes; three is even better: small, medium, and large.

Grater

Knives — small paring; French chef's
Get good-quality knives.

Loaf pan — 9" x 5"

Measuring cups

Measuring spoons

Mixing bowls — See *Bowls.*

Muffin tins

Oven mitts or pot holders

Pie plate

Potato masher — This is also useful for dicing a large quantity of boiled eggs should you be making egg salad sandwiches.

Pots or saucepans — small; medium; large

Rolling pin

Salad bowl

Spatulas — rubber; metal

Spoons — wooden; slotted; long-handled metal

Vegetable peeler — This may be used to core apples as well.

Not Essential, But Helpful

Blender or food processor
(Go for the food processor — beg, borrow, or steal if necessary.)

Cake pan — 8″ round
You will need two of these to make a layer cake. You may want to buy an angel food cake pan, but all of the recipes in this book may be baked in square or oblong pans. (See also *Baking pans*.)

Custard cups — Four is enough to start with.

Double boiler

Dutch oven

Egg slicer — This is handy for dicing eggs and slicing mushrooms. To dice eggs, turn lengthwise and then widthwise.

Electric mixer

Garlic press

Kitchen shears

Meat thermometer

Molds — 4-cup; 6-cup

Soufflé dish

Spring-form pan — 8″

Wire whisk

Wok

How to Measure

It is important that ingredients be measured properly.

Flour — Usually comes pre-sifted. Spoon it loosely into a dry measuring cup (no lip) and level it off with a straight-edged knife. Should you have only the liquid measuring cup (comes with a lip), make sure the flour is level.

Sugar — White sugar is treated the same as flour, but *brown sugar* is firmly packed.

All dry ingredients, i.e., baking powder, baking soda, salt, etc. — Be sure to use the proper measuring spoons and level off with a straight-edged knife.

Butter or margarine — It is helpful to know that most of these are marked in some way. If you buy the 1-lb. boxes, their contents are divided into four individual packages and each of these packages is 1/2 cup. If you need 1/4 cup, divide the package in half; should you need 1 cup, use two packages.

It is also helpful to remember the following measures:

2 tablespoons = 1/4 package

4 tablespoons = 1/2 package

8 tablespoons = 1 package

Authors' Note

We have mentioned many brand names throughout the book. This is not really an endorsement, as there are comparable brands available. These just happen to be our current favorites!

Index

Notes

Notes

GREAT COOKBOOKS FROM PRIMA

Prima's cookbooks are special. They have been carefully selected to be unique, attractive, and filled with great-tasting, easy-to-prepare recipes. To order, use the order form. Or ask for them at your favorite bookstore.

Slicing, Hooking, and Cooking by Jackie Eddy

Written by the co-author of the *Absolute Beginner's Cookbook*, this is a book filled with easy-to-prepare, make-ahead meals. Written for golfers, who are notorious for spending too much time on the green, this is a wonderful cookbook for anyone with a busy schedule.

Paperback Edition .... $ 9.95
Deluxe Cloth Edition $14.95

Lean & Luscious by Bobbie Hinman and Millie Snyder

This bestseller offers over 400 delicious recipes for today's low-fat lifestyle. Each recipe includes at-a-glance nutritional breakdown.

Spiral Comb-bound Edition $12.95
Hardcover Edition $22.95

Romantic Meals for Lovers by Gabrielle Kirschbaum

This beautiful cookbook is a collection of menus for 50 romantic occasions, from spring-time picnics to moonlit dinners. A wonderful gift or love offering.

Deluxe Paperback Edition $11.95

The Sicilian Gentleman's Cookbook by Don Baratta

Sicilian cooking is bold, simple, and delicious. With close to 200 recipes ranging from pasta to fish, this is the only Sicilian cookbook on the market. Interspersed with the wonderful recipes are hilarious observations by Baratta about Sicilians, the French, and other dubious characters (Americans included). Few are spared this light-hearted tongue-lashing. A one-of-a-kind book.

Deluxe Paperback $12.95

Absolute Beginner's Cookbook

Don't forget to order additional copies of this book for your friends and family. It also makes a terrific wedding gift!

Paperback $8.95

ORDER FORM

Please send me the following books:

Quantity	Title	Unit Price	Total
_____	_____	$ _____	$ _____
_____	_____	$ _____	$ _____
_____	_____	$ _____	$ _____
_____	_____	$ _____	$ _____
_____	_____	$ _____	$ _____
		SUBTOTAL	$ _____

6% SALES TAX (California only) .... $ _____

SHIPPING ($2 for the first book, $1 for each
   additional volume) .... $ _____

TOTAL ORDER .... $ _____

HOW TO ORDER: By Telephone: With Visa/MC, call (916) 624-5718
Mon-Fri, 9-4 PST (12-7 EST)

By Mail: Just fill out the information below and send with your remittance.

I am paying by (check one): ☐ Check ☐ Money Order ☐ Visa/MC

My name is _____

I live at _____

City _____ State _____ Zip _____

Visa/MC# _____ Exp. _____

Signature _____

PRIMA PUBLISHING
P.O. BOX 1260ABC
ROCKLIN, CALIFORNIA 95677
(Satisfaction unconditionally guaranteed)